As It Was Told To Me

MW00978232

As It Was Told To Me

Acts 27:25

Ted Theodore

Copyright © 2011 by Ted Theodore.

Library of Congress Control Number:		2011910706
ISBN:	Hardcover	978-1-4628-9581-6
	Softcover	978-1-4628-9580-9
	Ebook	978-1-4628-9582-3

All rights reserved. No part of this book may be reproduced or transmitted in any form or by any means, electronic or mechanical, including photocopying, recording, or by any information storage and retrieval system, without permission in writing from the copyright owner.

This book was printed in the United States of America.

To order additional copies of this book, contact:
Xlibris Corporation
0-800-644-6988
www.XlibrisPublishing.co.uk
Orders@XlibrisPublishing.co.uk
302147

INTRODUCTION

S HORTLY AFTER I affirmed Jesus as my personal Lord and Saviour, He through the Holy Spirit instructed me to start writing down the thoughts and wisdom He shared with me as I spent time in His presence. It was to be written in the moment, directly as I heard. Now, as I reach back to read them, I scarely believe I wrote some of them, but for my writing style and distinct handwriting!

This is the first in the series from those special personal moments. Come and be refreshed as we spent time together in His presence, hearing just as it was told to me.

ACKNOWLEDGEMENT

ONLY THE LORD, by His Spirit has made this possible! How can I ever truly thank you, Lord?I had the hand-written manuscripts, and for several years never took any further steps towards actually publishing it, until all the gentle goading became gentle proddings...

I acknowledge and thank my wife, friend and partner, Pastor Rachel Smith Theodore who has encouraged me the most on this journey as she has, on every other important step since she came into my life. Same thanks to Mayo and Jemimah, my wonderful and vey thoughtful teens, who in their own way egged me on.

Thank you, to all who have mentored me spiritually and physically, in my journey, especially those who have allowed the flourishing and expression of God's gift through me.

CONTENTS

THE REALITY OF A PROMISE

WHEN GOD PROMISES, rather when God speaks, His Word is certain. It is definite. It is truth. It is life. When Jesus said, 'The words that I speak are spirit and life', He was referring to the spiritual creation of the Word and the eventual physical manifestation. It is this certainty that makes the concordance meaning of the word 'promise', in the New Testament, come alive. *It means to anticipate (usually with all pleasure) confidence.* It is this certainty, assuredness, and confidence that Satan attacks and tries to distract in every way he can imagine. In Mark 4:17, the Bible says, 'When affliction or persecution ariseth for the word's sake, immediately they are offended'. The plan of Satan is to thwart our expectation, God's promise (John 10:10), and that is also why Christ was manifested to destroy the works of the devil (1 John 3:8). God's Word is true.

God cannot lie (Titus 1:2) so His promises, His Word, uttered are real. The Word of the Lord to you is perfect; His commandment is pure enlightening of the eyes (Ps. 19:7-9). We need to constantly place the Word before our eyes to enlighten us concerning His desires and His promises for us. This is what Paul wrote in Titus 1:9: 'Hold on to sound doctrine . . .' so that when persecution ariseth for the word's sake, the spirit of the Lord will raise up the Word as a standard against the devil's wiles.

Every promise of God for your life is a threat to Satan, just like every promise God made to His children from old. Matthew 11:12 tells us, 'And from the days of John the Baptist, the kingdom of God suffereth violence and the violent taketh it by force.' We have to be 'violent' in our belief of the manifestation of God's Word towards us—because He watches over His Word to perform it (Jer. 1:12) (Ezek. 12:25).

Every promise comes with a fulfilment time just as there is a time for every purpose on the earth. Sometimes, Satan's attack comes before the Word takes root. Sometimes it comes towards the fulfilment time of the promise. From the Garden of Eden, Satan has sought to thwart God's promise and to nullify its effect—sometimes with a substitute word, thought, or promise.

Especially when He knows that you know that, God cannot lie, but will do as He has said. Ezekiel 12:25 reminds us: "For I am the Lord; I will speak, and the word that I shall speak shall come to pass; for in your days will I say the word and will perform it," saith the Lord God.'

In the Garden of Eden, Satan started to attempt to steal God's Word from Eve, challenging her faith by asking, 'Has God said . . .' This was to get her to doubt what God had promised. It was the same strategy he used against her that he has used all through the ages, i.e. by seeking to divert our eyes and focus from the promises and Word of God and getting us to focus on the lust of the eyes, the lust of the flesh, and the pride of life. Even the temptation of Jesus was along these three areas.

When God promised Abraham a seed, Ishmael showed up and seemed to have everything that the promise would have, but real as it seemed, he was not the promise. Real as a manifestation may seem, it is not the same if it is not the promise. Hold fast to sound doctrine. Keep God's words before your eyes. As it is in heaven, so shall it be on the earth. Solomon built the temple, just like Moses built the tabernacle, based on specific instructions from God, who was particular about our purpose and the things He desired of and from us.

David was a key in the plan and promise of God, in the lineage of Jesus, also for the purpose of God for His people at that time. The lust of the flesh (focusing on what appeals to the flesh) almost caused his father not to put him up for selection because his other brothers looked physically 'more' like a king than he, David, did. But God insisted on his choice and purpose (of David as a king). On your day, God will insist on you!

Joseph's dream was nearing fulfilment, and Satan sensing that sent an 'easy' way through Potiphar's wife, who tempted him daily through the 'lust' of his flesh, eyes (probably exposing bodily parts), and pride (telling him how his status will change from a servant to the Master). Her temptation was daily, possibly several times daily.

Rehoboam made shields of brass to replace the gold (in the temple) which he lost when Shishak, king of Assyria, invaded Judah. Brass, when very well polished, looks like gold, but it is not gold. Hold fast to what you have heard (and read) as sound doctrine: what God promised He would do. According to Numbers 23:19, 'Hath He said, and shall He not do it?'

Jesus's birth was threatened by the killing of all two-year-old children. His life was targeted before His time, and when the final day came for His purpose to be fulfilled, Satan brought in a substitute—Barnabas, whose name also meant son of the father, just like Jesus was the Son of God.

WORRY NOT, BELIEVE!

JESUS SPOKE TO His disciples in Mark 11:24 that 'what things so ever ye desire, when ye pray, believe that ye receive them, and ye shall have them'. Therefore, indeed, if you believe that you have what you asked for, what sort of person ought you to be? What sort of thoughts should be on your mind about that thing? What sort of confession and profession should be proceeding from your lips?

The reason a lot of us worry about tomorrow and today is that we truly do not have that assurance that God is going to do as He has said. We have not truly internalised into our belief system what God's Word says. As a famous preacher once said, 'If you could peek into how your tomorrow would play out, the way God sees it, you would worry a lot less today.' Just imagine what you have already gone through (worrying about) and consider where you are today, what possessions (and peace) you now have, you would surely be ashamed (and should be) that you were so worried yesterday.

GOD HAS YOU ALL SORTED OUT

IN 1 SAMUEL 9, Saul is sent by his father to go with a servant to look for the lost asses. The fact that he had to go with a servant meant Saul was from a well-to-do family. That servant is for us today the Holy Spirit. For Jesus promised, 'I will never leave you comfortless: I will come to you' (John 14:18). In Saul's case, it was the servant who encouraged him to go and see the prophet Samuel. When you are lost and confused, it is God, through the ministry of the Holy Spirit, who shows you things (yet) to come (John 16:13). Listen to Him; talk to Him.

When Saul did therefore agree to go see the man of God, he knew he could not go without a gift. Even by today's standards, it is customary in all parts of the world that you usually take a gift along when you go and see a dignitary. A gift makes a way for you? The Book of Proverb tells us: 'However, for us believers, bringing a gift (to God) is like sowing a seed and bringing honour before God'. When you believe God has already answered, you will not hold back from being joyful and from sowing a seed. In some ways, when you pay for a car, a movie, or any service that requires payment before the actual experience of that service, it is like asking you to act or pay in faith knowing you will enjoy (satisfaction) more or equal to what you have paid for. That seed causes some obligation on the part of the receiver because by it you show the faith that 'I know my experience is going to be positive though I have not yet received it'.

Cornelius changed the plan and attitude of Peter (towards Gentiles). Cornelius gave so much that the Bible records in Acts 10 that his prayers and alms became a memorial before God. The apostles had to obey the heavenly order to go and get Cornelius's prayer answered. When you give generously, in faith, to God He will cause men to act on your behalf and in your favour. Cornelius kept on giving because he was certain that his prayers were answered and that God had come through. When God answers your prayers and men (like Peter) are hesitant about doing God's bidding, heaven will move on your behalf as it moved for Cornelius. In the case of blind

Bartimeus, he had worshipped Jesus proclaiming Him as the 'Son of God', declaring His faith and offering praises, yet the disciples tried to stop Jesus from responding to him—but Jesus responded. The disciples (and Peter in the case of Cornelius) behaved like Haman, attempting to stop Mordecai from getting decorated by the king. When you kneel before God, He will cause kings to show favour unto you.

Cornelius's faith is like, to me, a parent who watches through the window to see their son/daughter boasting to their playmates about what his or her parents can and will do for them. Surely, if only not to disgrace that child, the parent will move to act. God is watching to see your faith in action today—what will He see?

Saul finally meets Samuel in 1 Samuel 9:17, but even the day before, God had already spoken to Samuel about anointing Saul as king—Hallelujah! Here was Saul worrying about some missing asses, whereas God had greater plans for him.

As you obey God's Word today by doing what God commands—rejoicing and being thankful for answered prayers, as you sow in thanksgiving over what God has done (and will do), you will even begin to receive the greater things that God has put in store for you. Has He not said in 1 Corinthians 2:9 that 'eyes have not seen, nor ear heard, nor has entered into the heart of man, what God has laid in store for us'.

The 1 Samuel 9:16 says, 'Tomorrow about this time . . .' There are only about five to six times in scriptures that the Lord uses this phrase, and each time God uses it, He actually means tomorrow as in twenty-four hours. It signifies imminence—that God wants to do something *now*. In 2 Kings 7:1, Elijah tells the king of Israel that God was going to do something miraculous. He was going to end famine in a day and make food available all over. In that story, we again see the adviser of the king, another type of Haman, trying to stop the Word of God (through the prophet) from coming to pass by sowing disbelief into the king and those around the king. When God's advises, listen. Stand against God's Word and risk being shipped out or sent into oblivion like the king's adviser in 2 Kings 7.

Whilst Saul was yet worrying about the asses, they were found, and God had something else in store for him. God has finished the work, the table is set, your story has been concluded, and your future is assured. Jesus sits in victory atop all spiritual blessings in heavenly places. Do you believe your tomorrow will be specially blessed, that God has answered? Often, you could almost, genuinely, say so as we go through life and experiences. There are (or will be) moments of delight (and alas!) that really may give us a sense that we have reached the peak . . . that we know it all and have it all. It's like going to a high-class restaurant and eating some of the starters, which may be so delightful, and if you don't know, you could gorge yourself full when the main meal has not yet come. It is usually at this point that we say to ourselves . . . 'What could be better than this?' Curiously, there usually is something better in store for us by God!

YOU ARE NOT THERE YET

THAT YOU ARE not there yet means there is an original, predetermined destination. If there was no original destination, then 'there' could really be anywhere. For example, for the children of Reuben, Gad, and half the tribe of Manasseh, there was an original destination. There was a promise made by God, and this was clearly articulated to Moses as the Promised Land—the land of Canaan. In Joshua 1:11-15, Joshua reminded them of the promise that God made to them. In your situation today, there is a general command and promise made by God in Genesis for us to 'multiply, replenish, subdue, dominate, and possess the earth'. Also Christ promises us in John 10:10 that we should have life more abundantly! Specifically and individually, there is a promise or purpose that God has for each of us—that is usually expressed in what we want to achieve in life. To some of us, this is very clear, and to others, this is not so clear. Yet the lack of clarity and not being mindful of this vision often leads to suboptimal achievement.

> Never allow your present situation (pleasant though it may be)
> determine your destiny.
>
> (Num. 32:1-5)

On the way to your desired future, to your vision, there will be a lot of things that will appear pleasant and, dare I say, would be extremely pleasant. In this case, the two and a half tribes of Reuben, Gad, and half the tribe of Manasseh had a (genuine) need for fodder, but that need for the moment robbed them of the milk and honey of the Promised Land. For us, it may be the purchase of a car, a house, acquiring a degree, acknowledgement from people who hitherto would not look at us twice, etc., which may stop us from raising up our heads to see where God wants us to move on to next. This is the kind of behaviour the Bible called profanity in the case of Esau. The land that the tribes of Reuben, Gad, and half the tribe of Manasseh saw and desired was not given to them by God; it was Moses who, on seeing their profanity, allowed them to remain there. There are current successes or situations today that could be keeping you away from God's best. If you notice from reading more of that story, the children of Reuben, Gad, and half the tribe of Manasseh did not seem to have problems per se in the place they chose immediately; it looked like they had rest, so the presence of temporary rest or the fact that things are going well in a part of your life does not mean that you are there yet!

This is why Paul said to the Romans, in Romans 8:6-8, that to be carnally minded is death and to be spiritually minded is life and peace. Carnal minds look at today and the things that are visible, can be sensed, and explained, but the spiritual mind looks at things that are unseen, for the things that are seen are temporal. Lot looked and saw the pasture-rich land when he was to separate from Abraham. The land that looked like the Garden of Eden in Lot's eyes soon became (and was) the land of Sodom and Gomorrah. Therefore, like Abraham, set your affection and your mind on things above where Christ is seated (Col. 3:2) and press on for the mark of the high calling in Christ (Phil. 3:13-14).

The way out is to write that vision (God gave you) down; make it plain that all may run who read it. The Bible says in Hosea 4:6 that my people perish or are destroyed for lack of knowledge (not lack of ability or potential). When you forget or lose sight of your vision, then the present need and present success would determine your attitude and therefore your altitude. This is not in any way saying that you should despise your current success. No! No! Rather, thank God for them and let them be for you the proof that the same God that did this for you will complete the work He started (Phil. 1:6). This is why God told Joshua that the book of the law, pointing him to his future, should not depart from our face, our attention, our present—else the present would determine or, worse still, replace our destiny. Notice that the children of God, Reuben, etc. actually went into the Promised Land and did the work but did not partake of the inheritance. Why? Their focus was on something else. The problem with you today may not be the lack of effort or ability. It may simply be a lack of focus or desire for where God wants you to be.

GOD INDWELLING US

WHEN SOLOMON HAD completed the temple of God and was dedicating it, there was still in his mind a question about whether God would indeed dwell therein. Thus in 2 Chronicles 6:18, he asks, 'But will God in very deed dwell with men on the earth . . . ?' God wants to indwell us and wants to empower us to affect this world. Thus Paul says, 'I am crucified, yet I live and the life I now live, I live by the faith of the Son of God who died for me' (paraphrased Gal. 2:20).

When we begin to allow Christ to indwell and express His love through us, it is akin to what happened in 2 Chronicles 7:1-2. God's glory fills us just as at that time when the priests could not enter into the temple because of the glorious presence of the Lord. In the same way, no unclean thing, undesirable thing, or thought should come near or even inherit our bodies— God's temple. Rather from afar, other men will worship God, praising and thanking God, and be drawn to Him because of our dedication to Him. This will happen only when we are living sacrifices, when we live unto God and not unto men. It just thrills me to think of how even the priests could not enter the temple because God's glory had filled the temple. This holds a different meaning for us as believers in today's world.

Yes, indeed, God will come and dwell on earth and in man. That is why Jesus is also called Emmanuel—God with us. In John 14:23, Jesus has already said that 'if a man loves me, he will keep my words; and my father will love him, and we will come unto him and make our abode (dwelling place) with him'. When we obey His will, walk in His way, and keep His commandments, then we can truly know and be confident that He will hear our prayers and answer us. He has promised us as He did to Solomon also in 2 Chronicles 7:15 'that now my eyes shall be open and mine ears attentive to the prayer that is made in this place for I have chosen and sanctified this house that my name may be there forever'. The question is . . . has He chosen and sanctified you? If He sanctified you, today, then you need to allow Him/His glory truly indwell you (and cause your enemies and other worldly things to flee from you). Amen!

GOD IS LOOKING (I)

And Jesus entered into Jerusalem, and into the temple; and when he had *looked round about upon all things*, and now the eventide was come, he went out unto Bethany with the twelve.

(Mark 11:11)

IT IS MOST amazing that when Jesus made what is referred to as the triumphant entry into Jerusalem and into the temple, all that He did was to look! To think that He spent the whole day looking! But notice that He looked at everything—in other words *round-about-upon-all-things*. This means He spent time and was interested in every detail, looking at them from a multidimensional perspective. No wonder the Bible says we are not hidden from the eyes of Him with whom we have to do—our holy priest. Jesus wants to be glorified and wants to glorify God through us. So Jesus went to the temple to worship or for a very special visit (with the colt) and just spent the day 'looking'. Our bodies are temples of the living God, His dwelling place. Nobody buys a dwelling place without taking a continued and interested look. Sometimes (especially now in this Internet age), we even inspect hotels before we decide to stay or not. Jesus came to His figurative place of dwelling, and this showed that He was very interested in every part of the temple just as He is in our bodies and our lives today. It is worth considering a thought about what would Jesus find if He were to visit us today. He came riding through the praises and worship of the people—just as our praise and worship invites His presence into our lives, and when He does finally come in, what does He see? Praise and worship ushers Him into our lives, into our most inner selves, and what does He see? 2 Chronicles 6:9 says that God's eyes 'go to and fro the earth seeking to show Himself strong on the behalf of those whose hearts are perfect towards Him'. Isaiah says God's (eyes) searches the heart and tries the veins—that is how deeply God is interested in us. God is not just watching over us, He is also looking into us. David sang, 'Search my heart O God, see of there be any iniquity in me'.

GOD IS LOOKING (II)

Mark 11:12-13

THE FACT THAT He is looking and has expectations is then further manifested in the story of the fig tree. He was looking expecting that He might find anything thereon, anything, I might add, that would make a difference and would have ministered to Him or to His need at that time. So we see Jesus again looking deeply and finding nothing in the fig tree. Jesus must have passed that road and seen that fig several times possibly looking . . . and expecting and getting nothing, He answered, responding to the emptiness from the tree, 'With the measure you mete, shall men mete unto you'. Even today, Jesus is looking and expecting.

GOD IS LOOKING (III)

Mark 11:14

WHAT IS EVEN more amazing about this story is that Jesus, contrary to what we seem to think, did not curse the fig tree. The Bible says in Mark 11:14, 'And Jesus *answered* and said unto it, "No man eat fruit of the hereafter forever."' Jesus only answered or responded to a situation that was, as it were, 'taking' away from Him. Remember that He said that if you are not gathering with Him, you are scattering, which for me, in this circumstance, means that the fig tree was not adding value and over time had not. Jesus was teaching us there how to respond to situations that would want to destroy our hope—'for hope maketh not ashamed'. It was Peter who interpreted the response of Jesus to be a curse in 11:21, maybe because it was amazing to Peter that just a response, just something *someone* says, could be so powerful. I use *someone* deliberately even though I know that it was Jesus who said it because Jesus's response to Peter in 11:23 was that that same power and authority was available to everyone: thus He used the terminology '*whosoever*'. God wants us to respond to the dead, but lively looking things in our lives, things that may seem to add, rather really detract from us and cause our hope to be discouraged and disparaged. *Every word* we speak and believe is a creative and potent force for shaping the world around us.

GOD IS LOOKING (IV)—
CLEANSING IS NECESSARY

Mark 11:15

THE NEXT DAY, after Jesus had seen the temple, He returned to the temple and drove out everybody who was not supposed to be there. Jesus called the temple 'my house', meaning He knew what He was doing the day before when He was looking through the temple (house). One key purpose why He lives here in our bodies—His temple—is for our bodies to be called a 'house of prayers' so that all nations would testify to it by the fruit we bear. It is difficult to focus our prayers or even pray for that matter if we are filled with all sorts of clutter, all sorts of activities that hinder Christ from inhabiting and manifesting through us. You would notice that He could not minister on the first day and even on the second until He had purged the temple—our bodies, where He wants to dwell. He drove out everybody who bought and sold, i.e. every clutter and activity in us that keeps us from serving Him as we should.

KEEPING OUR THOUGHTS PURE

Mark 11:16

AFTER HE CLEANSED the temple, in 11:16, He did not allow any man who had vessels to pass through it. This means two things for me. The first is that, after cleansing, you need to keep your thoughts clean. This means not even allowing thoughts in or through us. Secondly, it means that as vessels of honour we carry or contain substance. Vessels specifically are mentioned here because vessels usually contain or have a potential to contain or carry material of some sort, which might contaminate or pollute our holy vessels. So for both reasons, He did not even allow them in.

THE POTENTIAL OF THE WORD

Mark 11:17

APART FROM AFFIRMING that our bodies are temples of the living God, He also said that we are houses of prayers. This means He wants to come in and commune with us; that is the purpose of His indwelling us. He was angry because they had made His temple a den of thieves. Thieves steal. They steal our joy, peace, fellowship, focus, etc., and that is why He passionately drove out the thieves. Today, He still wants to help us drive out the thieves in our lives. Thieves bring into homes pollutants that do not belong to the house, taking with them things that belong to that house. They make our bodies, God's temple, unsettled and deprive us of full fellowship and communion with God.

'In the beginning was the word and the word was with God and the word was God.' In a different way, you could say in the beginning was the Word/Sally and the Word was with Sally or vice versa, and Sally became the Word or began manifesting the attributes of God. Thus, the Psalmist says, 'Ye are gods', meaning the sons of God manifest the power of God on earth. In John 15:5, Jesus confirms this by saying that 'without me, ye can do nothing'.

It is the combination of the unity and the indwelling of the Word of God that makes Him Almighty. The Almighty God will not be God without the Word. We cannot accomplish or become anything without the force and efficacy of the Word in our lives. When God creates, it is through the creative force of the Word. When God created the earth, it was the Word at work. All of the foundation and creativity, rather the ability to change things and make a difference, the ability to dominate our world or circumstance is all founded in the connection between the Word and us. We are only able to make things happen, control our destiny, to the extent to which we allow the Word of God, the Word of life, and the Word of light indwell us and profess those words. In 1 John 4:4, the Bible says, '. . . and have overcome them; because greater is He that is in you, than he that is in the world'. We are only greater because the Word of God abides in us. When we are born again, we will usually have the potential to manifest God's power. Thereafter, we become sons of God, manifesting His power and glory, only to the extent that we allow the Word of God 'dwell with and in' us. When we first become born-again, we are like an electric generator that is not connected to a source of power. The Word connects us to the divine (power) grid—the power and presence of God.

It is further confirmed in His Word: 'If you abide in me, and my word abides in you, then ask what you will and it shall be done unto you.' It is that Word in you that brings with it a power to transform.

Is the Word with you? How much victory are you seeing in your life today? How much of His Word is indwelling you?

BRINGING INTO MANIFESTATION

I N THE STORY of the creation, especially in Genesis 1, one of the oft-used phrases was '. . . and God saw that it was good'. This was in reference to any aspect of creation that God just completed. When I think of that phrase by itself, it really does look sort of odd that God, our omniscient Father who knows the end from the beginning, should be seeing the work or creation for the first time and commenting on its beauty as it were. It looks odd to me because I am made in the image of God, and when I start pronouncing or declaring things that I want to happen, I usually would have seen those things in my mind's eye or the spirit, if you may. Just like when Jesus was here on earth, He said, 'I do only those things which I see my father in heaven do'. Therefore, before God spoke or created anything, He had seen them and believed them to be so before speaking. 'I believe, therefore I speak.'

God, therefore, in the story of the creation was not seeing for the first time that those things were beautiful or good. What I believe happened was this; indeed, before I go into what happened, if you look at the King James Version, the words 'it' was always in *italics*, which means they were not part of the original translation but were put in so the text could make sense when read in English. Therefore, what I believe happened was that after God created those items, He made sure they were perfect and were as good as what He had intended to create. As an excellent God and Father, He was setting an example for us, His children, to follow—which was to make sure that we looked to see and to perfect what we set forth or desire. As the Bible records, God watches over His Word to perform and perfect it. So when God speaks a word in your life, He does not stop there or move on to something else. He actually does watch over His promises to us to make sure they are fulfilled in our lives, just as He'd planned them to.

In fact, when God made man on the sixth day, He saw that it was very good; that is, God saw to it that His creation—man—made in His own likeness was very much what they as Trinity had intended. To this date, God is still interested in us, behaving as He intended and created—*very good*. This is His commitment to *quality* and *excellence*.

On the second day of creation (Gen. 1:6-8), God did not say (at least not as explicitly as in the other days) that 'it was good'. What was the reason for this? Creation was a process, and just as God did with creation, so He does with us today. So, though in Genesis 1:11, He had created the vegetation, we find in Genesis 2:5 that no shrub of the field had yet appeared. This tells me a couple of things:

a)   Though God created it already, He did not release the full 'throttle' because the keeper, man, had not been made on the third day. God would have us ready before allowing all the other conditions ready and necessary for our success to be made manifest and evident. Possibly the reason that it looks like those prerequisites are not in place yet is that God is still preparing us for our enthronement. Imagine how bushy and unwieldy the earth would have been with vegetation that no one needed. The manna and the quail remained only for as long it was necessary.

b)   In the process of creation, there was the creation step, which was God, pronouncing or calling into existence what was never there originally. The next step was about forming physically what was already created. We see this with man, vegetation, and the beasts of the field in Genesis 1:26 and Genesis 2:7; Genesis 1:11 and Genesis 2:9; and Genesis 1:24 and Genesis 1:25. What this means for me is that when I speak in faith, it is not enough to bring home. This means when we act in faith, we do not stop at the spiritual creation stage, but we go on to actualise what we have spoken into being by taking clear steps as God did in the creation story.

It was only after God had created man that He took him to the garden He had created for him. The garden was not the only place in the earth. The whole earth was already created when God planted the Garden of Eden. The Garden of Eden was actually a place that man was to enjoy and also hone his cultivation skills of dominion, replenishment, and fruitfulness (Gen. 2:15). God actually planted all the trees and vegetation in the garden, filling it with rivers of precious stones before man was brought in.

Every time God spoke about what He'd done each day during creation, the Bible records that '. . . and there was night and there was morning the second day' (Gen. 1:8). *What is striking is that the night always came before the day in those accounts.* What this should tell us, amongst the things, is that your morning is near, especially if you are passing through a night-time experience.

Adam and Eve saw in Genesis 3:6 that 'the fruit of the tree was good for food and pleasing to the eye . . .' That was God's intention when He planted the garden. The Bible actually records God's intention for all the trees in the garden in Genesis 2:9. The serpent's subtlety was in adding an additional thought about the tree of the knowledge of good and evil, making it seem like it was the only tree that had these attributes that God intended for the entire garden in Genesis 2:9. We see this from Eve's response in Genesis 3:6, suggesting that this was the only tree that had both good fruit and which looked pleasing to the eye.

What the devil did suggest though was that that tree was desirable for gaining wisdom. I think it was for this point that Eve took some and ate. How could she see that the fruit from a tree, just by looking at it, would make anyone gain wisdom? What happened was that the serpent sowed the thought into the head of Eve, who did not consult the original revelation and instruction of God.

Satan's strategy has always been to suggest thoughts that contradict God's Word. That is why we need (to rely on the Holy Spirit) to remember what God told us originally so that when those thoughts come, we can counter them with God's Word.

This is also why we need to evermore give more heed to the presence and personality of the Holy Spirit, who has promised to bring to remembrance to all that God has already spoken to us.

God wants us to have things that are pleasing to the eye and that are good for food. They need not be mutually exclusive. It does not need to look awful or bland to make it God's wish for us. The garden, the original habitation of man, was meant to be pleasing with the right things in the right places. Think of the placement of the river and how it flowed through the garden. God was the first designer, and there He showed the functionality of the design—it was both pleasant and good for food. Your house can look good and be very functional for living.

Hold on to God's original plan and purposes for you, and when in doubt or when unsure . . . go back to the scripture, which is able to save your soul!

ALL THINGS WORKETH FOR GOOD . . .

NOAH WAS A rare breed, a righteous man in the midst of an un-righteous world. It really would have required God's grace to remain righteous in that world, for where sin abounds, righteousness increases and grace abounds much more. Noah was he whom God chose when He was looking for a man to continue the lineage of Adam or man on earth.

One of the things about grace as well was that God gave grace to the work of building and preparing the ark. For example, Noah did not have to go around collecting the animals. God actually performed a miracle by asking the animals to come into the ark by themselves—imagine what it would have been like to have animals walking in, knowing where the ark was.

Walk and talk with God, then His grace will abound to you in every circumstance.

BLIND OBEDIENCE! ISN'T THAT FAITH?

Genesis 7

WHILST BUILDING THE ark, God told Noah to build a window. Noah, it was recorded, obeyed all of God's instructions, so he actually did build a window in the ark. When you think about it at the time, i.e. when he was building the ark (or today for that matter), there was really no reason for putting in a window if it was going to be raining all the time. Indeed, the earth was going to be flooded! The point is that we should obey God in spite of what we know or do not know, in spite of what we see or not, in spite of what the physical reality looks like! When we see what use that the window was put into later, it becomes a lot more obvious why God wanted it that way. In life we may or may not see why or who should do certain things or why we should obey certain rules that seem to have nil or a tangential-immediate relationship with what we are currently faced with.

At the basis of obedience to what may not be obvious or apparent to us is our trust for God and His Word. How can we trust someone with whom we have not, or as yet, spent so much time with? How can we trust the voice of Him with whom we rarely speak? We can only recognise the voice of those with whom we spend a lot of time. This is because we know them for who they are, what they say, and how they say it. God was angry with the children of Israel because they had seen the goodness of God severally; they had experienced His love and His deliverance for them; yet they still disobeyed or questioned His authority and His Word over and over again.

The window it was in the case of Noah that helped him and his family check when it was safe to open the door. Imagine what could have happened when he sent the raven out (and there was still water)? The ark would have been flooded if he had opened the door earlier; that would have meant that the entire purpose for building the ark would have been wasted because they'd have been flooded as well. What may seem insignificant, often, seemingly without a purpose, always with the Lord, has a purpose. *Trust Him; obey Him.*

NURTURE THE BENT

Even though every inclination of his heart is evil from child-hood.

(Gen. 8:21)

WHEN YOU LOOK at this scripture at face value, it does sound very child-unfriendly, when you consider that the child in today's world is often portrayed as innocent. However, to put things in perspective, where does a one- or two-year-old learn how to lie when he's standing next to a jam jar, with 'jammy' and sticky fingers, trying to playing innocent? Where does rebellion come from and at what stage in a child's life? Children indeed are vulnerable to all sorts, and that is why we need to specifically train them up to believe and love the Lord to secure their future. 'Train up a child in the way he should go and when he is old, he will not depart from it' (Prov. 22:6).

Necessarily, the verse does not say children are evil. What it actually refers to is the inclination, the tendency, the trajectory of a child's heart when it's untamed. The direction of the untamed heart is evil from childhood. Interestingly, in Proverbs 22:6, the phrase 'in the way he should go' comes from a root word that means or refers to a young shoot or plant that can bend in any direction depending on the wind or pressure put on it. What this verse means therefore is that very young children, who grow up without some form of direction, will naturally incline towards evil; like the young shoot which can incline in any direction, the unguarded and unguided human heart will incline towards evil from childhood. As parents, and guardians of the Lord's heritage, we have to steer the growth and development of the heart and mind of the child in the direction that the Lord has decided for that individual.

This is why child development is so important, especially when they are at an impressionable age. It stands to reason, therefore, why we see so much effort being made by the devil to steal the child's mind with all the video games, e.g. Harry Potter, Prince of Persia, Nintendo; TV shows, e.g. Disney shows; attraction parks, which do not, *to say the least,* promote the ideals and principles of the Bible. Subtly, they encourage children to look into themselves to be creative and imaginative without reference to the power of God inside us, which inspires that creativity. God is the Creator. He is creative and unimaginably imaginative. Believers should manifest creativity as Disney shows rightly allude to. The point of departure, from Disney shows, is the source of that inspiration and the acknowledgement of that source.

God want us to rise up to our responsibilities with children, nurturing them early for the Lord—especially in their infant years.

BLESSINGS IN A SEED

Genesis 9:1

GOD BLESSED NOAH and his sons; that is, God empowered them to prosper, saying to them or commissioning them as it were to be fruitful and to increase in numbers and fill the earth. This was the same commission He gave to man (spirit) after He created man (Gen. 1:28). When God want us to be blessed, He empowers us. The way He empowers us is through the principle of being fruitful and therefore increasing in numbers upon the earth. Being fruitful is at the end of a process. That process starts with sowing seeds.

To go further, let's look at both Genesis 1:28 and Genesis 9:1. They follow the same pattern; that is, God blessed them and said unto them or God blessed them (by) saying unto them. This again is a two-part process. There is empowerment—the state of being blessed—and there is the process of activating, enabling that empowerment, which God speaks unto them.

Blessings are really not a stand-alone thing. Even in today's world, when you have an empowered organisation, it means you have put in place a process or have articulated very clearly how people can be empowered. In truth, the organisations that are truly empowered are those that have people who have enabled themselves to make a difference. Merely saying that we are blessed without us enabling or activating that blessing is why sometimes as believers we don't (fully) see the manifestation of those blessings.

It seems they often so quickly forget what God said to them after He blessed (empowered) them. As I mentioned earlier, the process of enabling and activating the blessing (and the fullness thereof) of God starts with sowing seeds. The more seeds you sow (into fertile grounds), the more fruitful you are and, therefore, the more likely it is that you will increase, dominate the earth, and replenish it. If we take the case of mankind, unless man sows a seed into a (fertile) woman or indeed sows a fertile seed into a fertile woman, procreation or fruitfulness never happens in a family. Every increase starts from a seed.

When we say this or that family was blessed with a baby, what we are in essence saying is that they have enabled or activated the empowerment (blessing) of God by starting the process—sowing seeds, herb-bearing seeds (Gen. 1:29).

Therefore, to the extent that we sow seeds are we fulfilled and blessed. This is why it is more than perversion when we see increasing acts of homosexuality and abortion—it really is the devil trying to stop the enablement and activation of life and hinder fruitfulness upon the earth. It is to stop mankind—God's creation. Just imagine if everyone were a homosexual, then in a few years the world would cease to be and the life that God created, the first command and more so the expression of the ultimate commission of man on earth, would be stopped and defeated. This is why God was so angry at Sodom and Gomorrah and also with Onan, who spilled his seed or semen on the ground (Gen. 38:9-10). In Onan's case though, it was more than just a seed; it was the lineage of Jesus through Judah, which was at the risk of being threatened.

Seed in any and every form is precious to God for the life of the fruit; the future of any race, plant, or animal is in the seed. Destroy seed in any form and life is destroyed. To walk in the fullness of God's blessings is to be fruitful through sowing. That is why as sure as there is day and night, summer and winter, as long as the earth remains, seed time and harvest will never cease (Gen. 8:22). Indeed it is a mutually reinforcing principle because if seed time and harvest were to cease, then the earth would not last for very long. It's like a house without life or living inhabitants. After a while, that house begins to decay and disintegrate.

We can see the impact of natural fruitfulness in certain parts of today's Europe—the impact of homosexually and quite a few people's unwillingness to procreate and have children. Some villages are virtually going off the map because no children—no fruits—have been experienced in the last forty years. Around the horn of Africa—Eritrea, Sudan, Somalia, etc.—countless lives have been lost because of famine; the ground has 'refused' to reproduce or support sowing seeds. Seed sowing was the way God planned to perpetuate the earth. From one man Adam, the whole earth come forth; Abraham and Sarah created a new generation, and we all came from the seed (of the spiritual lineage) of Christ. Imagine that!

When the Bible says that God is delighted in the prosperity of His servants, it is because of this very fact—the increase we bring upon the earth. God is delighted because we activate His blessings upon earth. Jesus Christ was unhappy with the 'wicked and slothful' servant because he did not sow or increase the seed he was given; rather he kept what he had been given. Paul said to the Philippians (Phil. 4:17) that he was not seeking an increase for himself, rather for their own good. This is because as they sow into other people's lives, that increase into the lives of others excites God and so does their harvest (reaping). It is so exciting and important to God that He, personally, is in charge of the growth and multiplication process of the seeds once sown: '. . . God gives the increase' (1 Cor. 3:7).

In obedience to God, the first act or one of the first acts of Noah (as recorded in the Bible), in Genesis 9:20, was to plant a vineyard. In Genesis 10:1, we are told of the fruitfulness of Noah's family, procreating and increasing mankind upon the earth.

God is pleased when we sow seeds—of money, thoughts, good works, etc. especially when we consciously do it in recognition of the activation of our empowerment by Him—then He truly takes pleasure in our prosperity.

When you are blessed, it means you are fortunate to be *envied*. Why would you be *envied* if there were no signs of fruitfulness or of the manifestation of enabling or activating God's blessings? People will not envy you when they do not see proof of good things in your life. Man looks at the outward, so what is important to man is that they see the blessings, not just to hear you say you are blessed without any evidence of it. The evidence starts with sowing: '. . . and as long as the earth remains, seedtime and harvest will never cease'. Everything God created was in the seed form or was created with a seeding process. Jesus, the Living Word, without whom nothing was made that was made, came as a seed. Faith, by which we please God, came as a seed from God's Word. Sowing is so central to God's purpose for man on earth.

DISCRETION PAYS!

Genesis 9:20

NOAH BECAME DRUNK and was lying down in his tent. Ham, we are told, saw his father's nakedness. Whether he did that intuitively or not is not very clear and has not been given so much mention thereafter. What is really clear is that Noah was not pleased when he heard Ham saw his nakedness (when he was drunk) and told his brothers. A couple of life lessons can be drawn from this story.

The first is the importance of discretion. When Ham saw Noah, he was not discreet about it. He probably told his brothers and also to be 'discreet'; he then told them to 'keep it only to themselves'. This, of course, was not being discreet. Often we still get caught in Ham's same trap of carrying news from place to place—whether they are true or false is irrelevant. God wants us to be discreet and to manage the information we see and hear in a discreet manner, unless He wants us to do otherwise.

Proverbs 2:11 tells us that discretion protects. Often discretion and knowledge are tied together, e.g. in Proverbs 1:4, 8:12, 5:2. What this means is that there are many things we would know and see in life, but we should not say about all of them; rather, we need not say all of them. Discretion guides; discretion protects. When we remain discreet, we can sometimes have more occasion to protect ourselves and others. When we remain discreet, we will often have more occasions to meditate and make sense of what we see. For example, Mary visited Elizabeth and heard a confirmation of what the angel said to her, but she was discreet. Jesus went to the temple at age twelve and was teaching (with wisdom), and they actually forgot about Him in the temple on their departure. When they came back for Him, it was the subject of conversations, but Mary kept these things in her heart. Mary was discreet. Discretion will bring and keep you before kings. Kings, people in authority, and important people like discreet people.

The second lesson from this story is that even after he saw his father's nakedness, he did not cover it. Rather, he chose to spread the word to his brothers. This is why Proverbs 1:4 speaks about discretion to the young. If he had, after seeing the nakedness, covered him, then he would have even been further blessed. It is not in what we do that we miss our blessings; it is often in what we do not do! We often happen upon or hear a story about a believer. We could decide to keep quiet and tell no one, we could decide to tell others about it (often guised as a prayer point or a brotherly/ sisterly concern), or we could decide to pray about it in our closet and support the person. This last option is the application of both wisdom and discretion. Like I mentioned earlier, there are a lot of things we could come to know and God would bring our way. It is how we handle it which would determine how much more or less we would see. Also, it is how we deal with the things we see and how we use the grace that is upon us to minister to those situations we hear about which determines the extent that God shares things with us.

The third lesson is actually from Noah himself. I would suspect that this instance of getting drunk was a new thing for Noah; that is, it was not a pattern for him get drunk, otherwise he probably would have known how to manage his indiscretion. I would surmise that this was new to Ham; thus his behaviour was possibly borne out of surprise. I also think Noah's reaction was not borne out of being ashamed for doing what was not very proper. He probably would not have wanted anyone to know about. If this was not Noah's habit to get drunk, what then caused him to do it? What causes us to get into things that otherwise we would not do? Sometimes it could be plain complacency or an overall feeling of being unconquerable. Noah had just accomplished so much, and that may have created for him a sense of being able to do all things. This is probably why the Bible says, 'Let him that thinks he is standing take heed, lest he falls' (1 Cor. 10:12). Our moments of great victory could be our moments of vulnerability. 'Wine is a mocker, strong drink, a brawler,' says Proverbs 20:1.

The effect of Noah's curse, as it were, was quite strong and potent. Canaan, Ham's son, became the father of the Canaanite tribes of the Jebusites, Hittites, etc. who went on to occupy God's Promised Land. They also spread into Sodom and Gomorrah. There was so much evil emanating from this tribe or curse. It is also telling that Ham did not appropriate God's blessing for Canaan, nor did Canaan tap into what was already available to his father and grandfather. It would seem that Canaan was also chosen for a particular reason; that is, there were already signs of not living right. The Philistines also come from this lineage of Canaan. Imagine what wars and opposition the Israelites had to go through with people who would have been (and were) their own kinsfolk. These battles were a lot about stopping one of the physical manifestations of the curse so that they would not serve Israel as slaves. Canaan or Ham for that matter could have cried out to God, could have repented, and could have asked for mercy from God and his father, but it does seem they did so. Rather, iniquity multiplied and recourse was made to wars and battles in a bid to rid and free themselves from the manifestation of God's Word in later years.

When we go against God's laws we can, like David, ask for mercy. When we are dealt a hand, which is because of our association with a lineage, we can ask God to reverse the (negative) trend, like Jabez did. All hope is not lost because there is a curse against you. God's mercy is new each day (Lam. 3:22).

WHAT PATTERN ARE YOU BUILDING TO?

And by these were the nations divided in the earth after the flood.

(Gen. 10:32)

GOD'S ORIGINAL PLAN for the earth was to have Adam increase and replenish the earth according to the pattern he was shown. The model for increasing or spreading out from the Garden of Eden was in the garden itself. Just as in the case of building the ark and the temple, God's intention and plan was for them to build according to the pattern that He had shown to them.

There was a reason for God planting a garden for man to dwell in. This was the model of beauty, of perfection, which He wanted for the earth. It is just like how you can identify which colonial power had been in a part of the earth . . . . It is about the kind of houses and structures that would characterise that part of the earth or country. People would normally build houses based on what they are used to. The plan of God was for Adam and indeed all of mankind that the earth be as the Garden of Eden. Anything short of that was not acceptable. However, Adam's infamous expulsion from the garden also therefore affected whatever structures men built as they spread out all over the earth. The Garden of Eden was just a pattern, a model, so that when Adam's family grew, they would have had to expand all over the earth with the Eden model.

What Pattern Are You Building to?

LOOK BEYOND THE OBVIOUS

Genesis 11

TO MAKE SURE the expansion and spreading of man upon the earth was seamless, they all had to speak one language and keep in touch with each other. In the story of the tower of Babel, my impression was always that God confused their language because they wanted to build towers that reached the heaven. However, looking at it from a perspective of God's blessing . . . i.e. replenish the earth, sow seeds and multiply, have dominion . . . etc., man was meant to spread out all over the earth.

One of the implications of constructing the tower of Babel was that all of the earth was going to now be in one place. Genesis 11:4c confirms this: '. . . so that we may make a name for ourselves and not be scattered over the face of the earth'.

The tower was therefore a very deliberate act and a plan to go against the purpose of God for dominating and subduing the earth. It was also a thing of pride for men to build the tower. How much destruction pride wreaks in us. No wonder the Bible says, 'God is spirit'. It is a self-worship phenomenon. Pride looks inwards and seeks to glorify itself instead of God. It is the meek (not the greedy) who will inherit or possess the earth (Matt. 5:5).

Disobedience and pride in combination were the key drivers behind the building of the tower. God did not confuse their language just for the sake of it, but in doing so, He also made a way for His plan of men spreading all over the earth to come to pass for: '. . . the earth He has given to the sons of men'. According to Genesis 11:8, 'So the Lord scattered them from there over all the earth'. Genesis 11:9c says, 'From there the Lord scattered them over the face of the whole earth'. God will accomplish His purpose, despite the intentions of Satan trying to influence man to the contrary. This is why the prophet Jeremiah declares that God is watching over His world, to perfect it, to bring it to pass (Jer. 1:12).

OBEY IN PARTS, OBEY IN WHOLE

Genesis 12:1-3

GOD TOLD ABRAHAM, 'Leave your country, your people and your father's household and go to the land I will show you . . .' When I read and meditate on these words, it is obvious to me that to walk with God and to inherit Abraham's blessings, we truly in the practical sense of it have to walk with God and deeply trust Him.

Imagine being asked to leave where you have grown up with people you know, the work or profession you live off, the things you have trusted in life . . . and to go to a place that is nameless and unfamiliar. The only thing to look forward to is the promise, which if you could put yourself in Abraham's shoes and context (in time) would have to be a leap of faith. Here Abraham, or Abram as he was then called, had no child and was told he was going to be father of many nations—great nations, to be precise. His wife Sara was also barren! Against all of these odds, Abraham believed and hoped, against all hope believed even though there was little to hold on to, and believed even though people around him must have jeered at him.

Doing exploits for God's glory requires full faith in Him, suspending our beliefs and following His Word and direction every day, even today. There are places that God will have us go, things He'll have us do, and people He'll have us interact with and/or dissociate from; they may and need not make sense. They may not sound credible to us and especially to others. For it was meant for us, not them. It's like tasting food or taking drink and recommending, or not, to others. The fact that the food matched with our palate at that time does not mean that it would taste good to others. When people expect us to enjoy an experience because they enjoyed an experience, it does not automatically translate into an experience that is good for us. Great food might not taste great on every palate. What this means is that when God asks you to do something or go somewhere, it may sound strange to others, but that is what might differentiate you and indeed make His glory to be obvious to you.

It is very tempting, indeed comforting, for us to wait, to stay in, with those that we have always known. Departing from our place of necessary comfort to a place that has no links to or reminds us of the past can be a real challenge. This may explain Abraham's tie to Lot and his reluctance to let go of him amongst other reasons.

Where is God asking you to go today? What is He asking you to do/stop doing today? Can you and are you able to hear Him speak to you today? Have you been faithful in little? Do you (still) tremble at His Word?

LEADERSHIP 101

Bring to me 70 of Israel's elders, who are known to you as leaders
and officials among the people.

(Num. 11:16)

GOD TOLD MOSES these words when the first appointment of
leaders or an extended leadership team, as we would now know it,
was made. What is of more interest to me here is that the main criteria for
selecting these people were that Moses should know them as leaders! What
will distinguish you as a leader is what you do on a daily basis and not what
you do when you are appointed. Leading or showing leadership abilities is
important and key if we were to fulfil God's commandment of dominating
the earth, subduing of, and multiplying upon the earth.

To be sure, it is not just when we 'lead' people that we show leadership.
We actually show a lot more leadership when we live in line with God's words
or ideas, to use today's corporate parlance. Our ideas and the underlying
values should be consistent and be seen in our behaviour each day. These
folks chosen as leaders did not set out, I hope, to show leadership because
they wanted to be chosen because hitherto these had never been a selection
of leaders; that is, people had never been formally chosen.

What this means for me is that we must on a daily basis *make a 'leadership'
difference to people* because if people do not feel the impact of our leadership,
then it will be challenging for us to be formally picked as leaders. *Leadership,
I dare say, is an attitude, not a role, not an appointment.* Moses only formally
recognised them and put some authority in their role. Long before this
time, they were already leaders in every sense. Are you leading today? And
how is that so?

CYCLES OF LIFE (BLESSINGS)

As long as the earth endures, seedtime and harvest, cold and heat, summer and winter, day and night will never cease.

(Gen. 8:22)

THE CERTAINTY IN Genesis 8:22 and Luke 6:38—'. . . shall be given unto us full measure, shaken down . . .'—stems from a cyclical principle that God has put into place and is a key determinant in the existence of mankind. We build our world very much around the fact that there is a morning after the night and vice versa. We plan for winter whilst basking in summer. We endure winter because we know summer is only a couple of months away. *How come we are so certain about day and night, summer and winter, but are not so certain and, indeed, do not build our lives around the principles of seed time and harvest?*

One of the key things about these four cycles of nature, God's timeless principles, as I now call them is that they are all seasonal and are time-bound. It was never God's intention that you would only keep on sowing and never reap. Neither was it God's intention that we would be only harvesting (and sometimes the wrong things) continually. This is the other key thing to note. Seed time results in harvest, and harvest gives us seeds to plant at seed time. Therefore as said before, seed time will only last for a while, but surely thereafter comes harvest. Even the principles of business are driven by this nature. There is time to work . . . and there is the pay check at the end of the week/month—harvest. Thus, because they are related, a causeless curse shall not come. This means if anyone wants to put a curse on your harvest, the only way that can happen is if you have, during seed time, given others a cause to be able to stop your harvest, maybe by breaking the hedge. You can create a new harvest for your tomorrow by sowing a seed of righteousness today (Hos. 10:12). Job said, 'Though your beginning be little (small), your latter end shall greatly increase.' This is a statement for the principle of seed time and harvest.

The only way your future will be different is if you do something today during seed time. What are you sowing today in your thought life? Are you sowing thoughts like Job's—i.e. 'The thing that I feared not has come upon me?' You can sow all sorts of things and not just money. The key is to ask yourself what you want your harvest to look like, and based on that, you can then sow a seed. It could be seed of peace, trouble, love, patience, etc. When you see things happening to people and people going through some experiences today, it is almost down to a seed that they sowed or did not sow during seed time. The key thing is to *not* allow and reflect and remain where you are today . . . . Sow seeds and change your tomorrow! Take advantage of the continuous seed time (and harvest). Take advantage of the seed time (crucifixion) and harvest (resurrection of Jesus and the church today).

One interesting thing about seed time and harvest is that the amount of seed we sow is not arithmetically related to the amount of harvest we reap, especially if we have sowed on good ground at the right conditions. Hosea 8:7 tells us that even when we sow the wind, we will reap a whirlwind—an increase. Paul in 2 Corinthians 9:6 says that we should sow generously to reap generously. Luke 6:38 tells us that men will give to our bosom, pressed down, shaken together. All we need to do is sow, and the reason it multiples (if we do it correctly) is that it is God who gives the increase (1 Cor. 3:6-7). Harvest will always come after seed time. Look at the story of Joshua's election; Jacob and Laban; Abraham and the Israelites; Isaac and the hundredfold return; and of course, Jesus and us. Jesus was laid to the cross and triumphed over hell and the grave, becoming a sinner for us so that we might become the righteousness of God. God sowed during seed time because He knew that as long as the earth remains, there would be a time for seeds (after which it may go bad) and time for harvest.

Rejoice because you can sow in tears today, but tomorrow you will doubtlessly come in bringing or reaping in the sheaves with joy. Psalm 126:5-6 says that it may look like it is taking a while, but wait for it. It may look like the seed has died; yes, the seed has to die first for it to bear fruit. *Ironically sometimes we never let the seed die* and therefore never see the harvest. We unknowingly keep the seed alive by talking or complaining about it, in the process uprooting the seed. The latter we do by asking what happened or is happening to the money or seed we sowed. We sow money into the church or into someone's life and keep on wondering what they have done with the money. By doing this, we keep our ties to the money, keeping it alive, instead of letting it go so that it can bear fruit. This is often why we do not get the results and harvests we desire.

Instead of giving in to murmuring, etc., once you have sown in seed time, we should recognise and practise the principle of daily thanking God for the harvest we expect.

GROWTH

AS YOU LOOK forward to summer, to the evening, or the next day, surely look forward to your harvest, and let that consciousness drive how you use your seed time today and in the now because Galatians 6:7 says, 'You shall reap what you sow'.

Growth is a word or terminology that is synonymous with increase. It means moving from one stage (a lower stage) to a higher level stage or phase in life. Growth is key to God's plan and purpose for the earth. It is evident from the creation story that God made/created things in or with their seed form—the way to increase and multiplication is through growth, from a lesser form to a higher one, often from a seed.

The first commandment or instruction to man, in fact, you may appropriately call it a job description, was in Genesis 1:28 when God told them to 'be fruitful and increase in numbers, fill the earth and subdue it . . .'

In Genesis 1:29, He said, 'I give you every seed-bearing plant on the face of the whole earth and every tree that has fruit in it . . .' So, clearly, God was setting the standard for how we should live our lives and how we should increase and dominate the earth.

God's plan for us is to increase us. Just to make that more explicit, look at the story of Jesus. In Luke 2:52, the Bible tells us that Jesus grew in wisdom, in stature, and in favour with God and man. This (Luke 2:52) is the epitome of growth—a four-dimensional model which covers every aspect of our lives. If we want to be impactful, the way our Lord Jesus Christ was, then we need to focus our attention on these four areas of our lives. What do they specifically mean?

Growing in wisdom refers to our *intellectual capacity*. This is not just in getting educational qualification, but it is in the application of knowledge in such a way that it impacts the lives of those around us and situations around. When Jesus was twelve years old, He could already sit with and marvel teachers of the law. He had, and showed, so much wisdom that people marvelled at Him. This is God's plan and hope for us—that we should show forth wisdom and that this wisdom would be made manifest to all. Daniel's wisdom was manifest for all to see. With each king and each situation that came, it was clear that there was a spirit of wisdom and excellence operating in his life. It was not a one-season wonder. It was not something that was here, and lo! It was gone tomorrow. It was not only there . . . it actually grew.

The second dimension of growth is growing *in stature. This is physical growth.* We are born little, tiny, and weenie, but that is not how God wants us to remain. Jesus grew in stature; that is why He could do all the long walks, help His father as a carpenter, etc. Growing physically has very little to do with just height and weight. At a point in our lives, we obviously need to manifestly grow in stature. This means we can actually believe that we would get to a point in life, an age, where we no longer (need to, hopefully) grow just in size.

Physical growth or growth in stature also happens internally. Every day and possibly many times daily, we regrow our cells, our blood is renewed, etc. It is this internal growth and rejuvenation of our cells that really manifest in the outward growth we see. For example, to grow bigger muscles, what often happens is that when we exercise, the old muscle actually tears up, and it is only when we keep on exercising and eating the right kind of food that the regrowth process starts and an even newer and bigger muscle—biceps—develops or emerges. As in all of the dimensions of growth, we do have a part to play to ensure that we do indeed grow. That it is God's intention is not in doubt; however, we need to activate our faith and growth by active obedience. Physical growth is what the Bible refers to when it says, 'God fills our mouth with good things; so that our youth is renewed as an eagle's'. Good things, renewal, the physical growth of the body happen every day to every living person because the day you stop growing is the day you start dying. That Jesus grew in stature also meant there was no disease, not a whiff of ill-health in Him that could and/or did affect His physical mortality and well-being.

The third dimension of growth is the *spiritual dimension.* The Bible tells us that Jesus 'grew in stature and in favour with God . . .' Again, maybe it is worthwhile to expound a little on the word 'grow'. To grow means to increase, and this growth could be multidimensional; for example, it may mean horizontally, diagonally, vertically, and even downwards to take root: '. . . being rooted and grounded in love that ye may be able to know what is that good, perfect and acceptable will of God' (Eph. 3:17). So growth in favour with God can really be beyond our imagination; that is, how do we grow or increase in favour with God continually? If we look at the life of Jesus and also other men whom God used, it is very obvious that they grew in favour with God . . . as they walked with God.

As with the other dimensions of growth, increasing in favour with God comes from spending time and being obedient to the will of God. Jesus was wholly and totally obedient to the will of God and therefore increased in favour with God. 'This is my beloved Son in Whom I am well pleased.' The psalmist says, 'God daily loads us with benefits.' 'His mercies towards us are new each day.' 'He has bedecked us with favour as a shield.'

This spiritual dimension, so to speak, very much dominates how we increase or grow in the other dimensions. For example, Proverbs tells us that if a man pleases God, i.e. if our way of life finds favour from God, God will cause even our enemies to be at peace with us—that is, we will find favour with men. As we increase in God's favour, so does wisdom; God's wisdom increases in us also. When our desire is to please God rather than men, God will cause men to be favourable towards us. After all, the king's heart is like a stream in the hand of the Lord, and He, God, will direct it whichever way he pleases (Prov. 21:1).

Just as the other dimensions of growth are dependent on our obedience of God's Word, so also is spiritual growth or growing in favour with God. Obedience means we hear/listen to God's Word, and we actually do it. Our ways will only please God if we do His will. James tells us to be doers of the Word and not hearers only, and we should show our faith by our works.

The fourth dimension of growth that we should be experiencing is that of *favour with men*. This means that as we increase in favour with God, we would increase daily in favour with men; that is, it may be the same people, but their favour towards us would increase. This is daily because Psalm 103 tells us that God daily loads us with benefits—favour is a benefit.

So we could say the first dimension of growing spiritually (with God) is vertically upwards.

The second dimension of growing in favour is horizontal—having favour with more people. God's plan for us is that, as we remain in His will, He will cause more people to have favour with us. Daniel experienced such multiple and continuous favour with several kings of Babylon who he had to serve. Joseph had favour with Potiphar inside the prison and with the Pharaoh. Jesus increased in favour with men, not just men. If we are indeed going to increase upon the earth, then we need God to touch the hearts of kings to open doors for us.

The third dimension of favour is really exponential or diagonal in its manifestation. We will increase in favour in more dimensions with more people at the same time. In a sense, it is a mix of the first two. This is God's plan for us.

There is a relationship amongst these four dimensions. As we increase in favour with God, He gives us wisdom; wisdom gets us favour with men. As God renews our youth as the eagle, men (who always look on the outwards) will show us more favour. As God gives and increases us with favour before man, so kings will give us access to situations that will cause us to grow in wisdom and consequently increase in favour with those kings/men.

Growth, increase, is God's plan. We need to look forward each day to growth opportunities . . . because it is God's plan for us. Jesus came to show us the *way*.

J ESUS, IN RESPONSE to the Jews as to how He could show a miraculous sign to prove who He was or had authority to do what He did at the temple, responded that He would destroy the temple and rebuild it in three days. There are two key lessons for me from this conversation.

The first is that no matter how long it takes for you to build your 'life' out of Christ, He can rebuild it in three days, if only you allow Him access into those things you cherish the most but are not of Him.

The second lesson, which comes from verse 22, is that Jesus is merciful towards us, and our 'unfaithfulness' towards Him would not change His faithfulness towards us. In verse 22, the Bible tells us that the disciples who had walked with Him and seen diverse manifestation of His divinity and power did not believe the words that He spoke there. It was only after His death and resurrection that they did.

What this also means is that people around us may not believe everything we say because they cannot see the vision we see, but that should not stop us from implementing what God tells us. It's like the proverb that says that despite the fact that we sleep on the same bed, we should not expect of a necessity of having the same dreams or understanding each other's dreams. People, not just the disciples, did not believe Jesus until after the resurrection, but Jesus still kept faith with them, i.e. the disciples. Sometimes the fact that people do not see what you see/say means you are operating at a different level. Just make sure that like Jesus, you are doing only what the Father has shown you, that you are building according to the pattern . . . in which case, just plod on.

SOME (PRAYER) 'BACKING' USUALLY HELPS

Daniel 2

DANIEL WAS IN a situation where he had to respond to a challenge that was not brought on directly by his behaviour. The king had asked his 'usual' wise men to interpret a dream that he had. They could not, and he then ordered that all the wise men in the land should be killed.

In Daniel 2:9, the king acknowledges that the so-called wise men were really con men just hoping things/fortune would favour them. If in your office, school, church, or wherever you are, there are people that you know who 'major' in eye service and are short on delivery, do not worry because one day God will expose their trickery and your wisdom shall come forth. The king knew all this time that he was being bilked, so the fact that the king in your case is not reacting against these unfaithful workers should not get you discouraged. 'Work as unto the Lord.'

When the wise man asked for extra time to reason out the dream, the king refused. However, when Daniel asked for extra time even after the pronouncement of death to all the wise men in the land, he was given some extra/additional time (Dan. 2:16). The same king who had said 'no' to a request by the regular wise men for extra time said 'yes'; the same king who had issued an execution order waived it for the season, in fact granted him an audience! This was just like when Esther went to see the king at a time when the king did not welcome women.

Daniel did not do this alone. In Daniel 2:17-18, he went to his friends in faith—the other three Hebrew wise men—because if two of you shall agree concerning a thing, it shall be done for you. Go to people of faith and of like mind. Use the resources you have. They prayed a prayer of agreement and God responded.

When God responds, give Him glory. In Daniel 2:26, when the king asked Daniel, 'Are you able to tell me my dream and interpret it?'

Daniel's response was 'But there is a God in heaven who reveals mysteries . . .'

Give God the glory because without Him we can do nothing.

GET UP! GO BACK!

Remain humble! Daniel was humble; thus, he asked his friends to pray with him and gave glory to God. Use wisdom and facts in your engagements

(Dan. 2:14b).

IN ZECHARIAH 1:3, the prophet prophesied to the people, saying, 'Return to me and I will return to you'. This is God's constant message to the church and to His children. 'I will never leave you, nor forsake you.' In 2 Timothy 2:13, the Bible tells us that if we are faithless, He will remain faithful, for He cannot disown himself. God will not wander away from us (His love); we are the ones who may get lost, and He is always faithful and does not walk away.

Thus, the Lord is confident to say, 'If you seek me, you will find me, and once you have found me, then knock on the door.' God wants us back where we left Him (if we did). When the text says 'I'll return to you', in reference to God, what it means is not a journey made, per se. It means all of God's love, mercy, and forgiveness will come back and be available to us. This is the message of restoration and promotion, just like the prodigal son.

Get up! Go back! Stop listening to the lies of the devil. God is waiting. Love is waiting. Mercy is waiting. The fatted calf, merriment gold rings are waiting for you!

It is just like when you stay in perfumed or odorised room for a while and thereafter you move out, and you no longer smell that odour/perfume. All you need to do to experience that smell is to get back into that room, and as it were, the smell/perfume will return to you. It is not as if the perfume went away. It is that we left God's presence.

God is always there. Always waiting, always loving, always kind.

LEADERSHIP ACCOUNTABILITY

SAMUEL DISPLAYED AND probably set the first example for 360-degree feedback for leaders at any level. There he was at the end of his reign as a judge, asking for feedback and willing to make right whatever wrong he might have done.

What was really commendable about the timing of this request was that he was on his way out of office, and therefore people could say their minds without fear of being 'hounded'. This was quite different from the tokenistic approach to feedback that we have come to see with some leaders. He was willing to show accountability, not just for himself to the people, but also before the Lord and the anointing of the Lord. This was genuine for him, and there was a real risk of losing his anointing if he was pretending.

One of the several things he asked for feedback on was that if he had taken a bribe to prevent justice, he was willing to make restitution for it. This demonstrates how high his moral standards were because this was one situation where the person defrauded by the perversion of justice could have easily cried out. But none did.

GOD IS OUR SOURCE

IN PROVERBS 1:11, the Bible cautions us not to lie in wait for people's blood, not to waylay some harmless soul. This statement may seem quite far-fetched for most folks, given the fact that they do not necessarily spill people's blood on a daily basis. However, when we gather with others either within or without the body of Christ and cast aspersions about people, about their character, about how they live their lives, then we are getting ready in effect to spill people's blood.

It does not matter what the circumstances are, we should not talk behind people's backs without them knowing, saying how terrible they are. When we do not give them feedback, we in effect seek directly or indirectly to destroy their future. It is about how our comments 'waylay' other folks, hoping that by destroying them (or pretending not to) and their reputation we can take what is theirs or stop them from being a threat (Prov. 1:10-19).

We should, as believers, be aware that our source is God, not man. We should be conscious of the power of God in our lives and that Jesus Christ is the same, yesterday, today, and forever (Heb. 13:8)! Let us not be drawn into that seat of scoffers and scoundrels and negate our faith by our actions/deeds. If we want wealth, position, or power, we should remember that it is God who makes our way perfect and who keeps our arm strong.

Our strategy for increase is biblical—giving, sowing, and reaping. It is not by *getting* all we can and *canning* all we can get/grab. Let us remember *continually* our source—*Jesus*. It is He that pulls down one and lifts up another—not our mouths or behaviour.

LOVING SIMPLICITY?

SIMPLICITY MAY MEAN several things to several people in several circumstances. In Proverbs 1:22, 32, we get a sense of the meaning of simplicity as I intend here, at least some direction of my thinking. Simplicity here means complacency, letting things go so easily, or not taking to heart or with any seriousness God's Word. A simple-minded person or a believer in this case is one who does not spend enough quality time trying to understand the richness and depths of wisdom behind God's Word.

Wisdom is deep. Wisdom requires some investment of time and belief that it is worth doing. Herein lies the folly of simplicity—not going deep enough. For a lot of believers, just getting by is just good enough, just knowing that they are saved. Even with the things of this world, e.g. professional knowledge, you only get to the true depths and appreciation of them when you spend quality time with the source of that knowledge. In fact, if you show any lacklustre attitude or some measure of disinterestedness, the professionals of this world will not reveal the deep insights to you.

Simplicity will get you by when there is no trouble, no attack, and no immediate distress, when depth is not required. Thus, where there is no depth immediately required, people might gravitate towards simplicity; therefore, their foundations are shallow and weak. This necessarily limits the extent of their achievement, especially if we liken this depth of our life/Christian foundation to the height of a building and the foundation it requires to successfully withstand at a particular height.

In Proverbs 1:33, wisdom declares that whoever listens (and thereby builds a foundation) will lie in safety and be at ease without fear of harm. Simplicity, taking life 'easy', exposes. Wisdom, paying attention, and storing up God's Word will cause us not to fear. Fear is evidence that you have become too simple, not taking into account the richness and might of God's grace. *Simplicity and complacency prevent us from going deep enough and make us miss the richness of drinking an unstirred cocoa drink.* Simplicity is akin to believing without meditation and asking for further revelation.

TED THEODORE

THE SHINING PATHWAY

The pathway of the righteous shineth brighter unto the perfect day.

(Prov. 4:18)

THIS MEANS OUR pathways, our walk with God, our lives, and our testimony upon the earth should be getting better with each day. Unlike the way of the world, the way of the Word is that things should get better with us with time and that just like wine gets more expensive with age, so we do with age. Like Job said, 'Though our beginning be small, our latter end shall greatly increase.' We increase with the increase of God.

This increase though does not just happen. It comes as a result of our previous actions. As with all of God's laws, increase comes because we have sown something into the kingdom. This is what causes us to reap. We need to sow God's Word daily into our hearts and our situations so that the increase and the continual brightness of the path of the righteous is not a fluke, nor just by confessing that verse of scripture alone.

In Proverbs 6:23 and Psalm 115:109, the Bible tells us that the Word of God is a lamp and a light that guides our lives and our paths, that the corrections of discipline are the way to life. Thus, the Word of God is the way to life—Jesus said in John 14:6 that 'I am the Way, the Truth and the Life'. Therefore, our pathways can only shine brighter as we walk in His Word and His pathway—in Jesus. We daily need to sow the Word of God into our lives; we need to daily meditate on the Word of God, thereby making our way prosperous.

Our pathway shines brighter and brighter because we illuminate it with the Word of God. The Word of God is an instructor—guided by the Holy Spirit who teaches us what to do, where to go. As we listen to and obey Him, the increase of peace and the reign of God's Word or Life (Zoe) upon us, shall never end. If we hide the Word of God in our hearts daily, then we cannot sin against God.

God's Word must be continually freshly sowed into our hearts to yield that ever-increasing and bright pathway for us as believers. Our lights will not dim because the Word, which lives forever, powers our light.

MAN

THE TEMPLE IN the Old Testament was the dwelling place of God's presence with His people. The temple had so much importance for God that the instruction on who should build it and how it should be built were very precise. David, for example, could not build it because he was a man of war, sullied with blood. There were instructions even on what items could be used inside the temple and what care should be given to them.

In the New Testament, there is no need for God to dwell any longer in a physical temple—albeit God's presence dwelt there—for God does not dwell in a temple made by human hands. We (our bodies) are the temple of the living God. God's spirit lives in us—in our bodies (1 Cor. 3:16-17, 1 Cor. 6:19-20, 2 Cor. 6:16). Our bodies are not our own. Our bodies are like a receptacle, holding something like a vessel. And like a vessel, it will hold whatever liquid you put into it.

Our spirit is what becomes alive when we are born again. Our bodies do not. So they still would want to function the way they have been for always. John 14:15-20 tells us about the indwelling spirit, about Emmanuel (God with us). As His children, God wants to commune with us (John 15).

We are spirits; we live in a body and we have a soul. Our spirit is our contact point with God's spirit; our soul is the conduit between the spirit and the body. The body is the contact point with the world. When we yield to God's world, we renew our mind (soul) to be in line with God's Word. Our mind is our source point with the world and therefore is the battleground (2 Cor. 10:4-6). Therefore, we have to guard our heart—guard the doorway (Prov. 4:20-23).

2 Chronicles 23:4-7 tells us about guarding our entrances. There are doorways that we must protect. When there is no temple, there is no vessel for the spirit to occupy. There are things that are corrosive to our vessel—the body. God's Word is a healer and a builder (Luke 6:45).

BE BLESSED IN YOUR STRENGTH

SOLOMON, THE TEACHER or Preacher as some translations will refer to him as, said in Ecclesiastes 2:24, 'A man can do nothing better than to eat and drink and find satisfaction in his work. This too I see is from the hand of God, for without Him, who can eat or find enjoyment.'

One of the challenges that most people, including Christians, find today is being able to find and do work that is satisfactory to them personally. Today, one of the latest thinking in developing and managing people is primarily focused on finding people's strengths and being able to give people roles that play according to their God-given or God-assigned purpose. Purpose is only found in the creator of a thing. Therefore, finding purpose and finding your strength and your potential is only attainable from walking and fellowshipping with God.

As Solomon rightly remarks, who can find enjoyment without God, or better contextualised, who can find out what they enjoy doing without God? It is God who gives that wisdom so that even though work may require a lot physically because we enjoy it and find it fulfilling, it does not become a dreary bore.

Even the geneticists would acknowledge and tell us that it is important to know that every person has a different genetic make-up and therefore will more readily be successful in some areas than others.

Also, in doing work and accomplishing success upon earth, as believers we are also confident that the memory of the righteous will be a blessing (Prov. 10:7). Therefore, we are confident that the result of our efforts—either when we finish a task and move on from here on earth or when we pass on to glory—will be a blessing. It will not be lost or thrown away and wasted as Solomon alludes to in Ecclesiastes 2:18-19.

Look to God for your strength, your purpose, and your calling and see the difference it makes for your career and productivity. God is the one who also will uphold your strength and will make your way perfect. Amen!

ADVERSITY AND FRIENDSHIPS

ADVERSITY AROUND YOU is no proof of God's distance. In Daniel 3:11, the Lord was in the fire with Daniel and his friends. God's presence was with David, throughout his travail with Saul. Psalm 23:4 tells us about God's presence in the valley of the shadow of death.

In Acts 12:6-7, there was a night when Peter was scheduled to be killed after James was murdered. The king still owned the courts and the prison; there seemed to be no hope. Friends are made for adversity (Acts 12:5, 12,17c; Prov. 17:17). Brethren and friends kept on praying for Peter. Jonathan never left David in times of his adversity, and David remembered Jonathan's family after his death. David remembered and married Abigail. In today's world, successful teams and companies are often built through shared adverse/difficult experiences. Daniel always called on his colleagues for support. Peter's brethren did not 'spill' during the search (Acts 12:19). You do not hope to have Job's friends (as they were in the beginning in times of adversity). Ecclesiastes 4:9-12 tells us that a three-fold cord is not easily broken—it's about the power of friendships and the Holy Spirit in this verse of scripture.

GOD WILL SHOW UP. WAIT FOR HIM

GOD WILL SHOW up (Acts 12:7). Wait for Him; remain obedient. God showed up in the lion's den and in the fire for Daniel. Saul at the point of frustration, looking for his lost asses, saw Samuel and the solution. Elisha proved to his servant that God's army was around/with them when they were surrounded. God kept Peter during the temptation and the three crows of the cock. Jesus found the coin in the fish's mouth when He had to pay tax. In the dead of the night and darkness, Jesus came through walking on the sea. God will show up—and deliver you (Isa. 49:24-25).

You just need to stay focused. Complete your course. Act wisely (Acts 12:8-11, 17). Whatever you are going through and wherever you are, keep your salvation with reverence and trembling. Run the race. Keep the faith; think pure and lovely thoughts, even in your dreams.

YOU MAY BE IN GOD'S WAY

GOD WILL AVENGE His enemies (Acts 12:19, 23-24). God promises that 'blessed are those who bless you and cursed those who curse you' (Num. 24:9). 'He who touches you touches the apple of my eye' (Zech. 2:8). 'Vengeance is mine. I will repay,' says the Lord. God is setting your enemies and those who stand up against you for failure. God says, 'Touch not my anointed, and do my prophets no harm' (1 Chron. 16:22).

> God is waiting for you to step back from your enemies so he can act against them—wait for Him. (Isa. 49:24-25)

> Are You Proud or Just Afraid? (1 Pet. 5:6-7)

Peter admonishes us to humble ourselves before the Lord so that the Lord will exalt us. He goes on further to say that we should cast our entire burden upon the Lord for He cares for us. In fact, the original translation of the word 'burden' is anxiety.

What is the cause of our anxiety? Why are we so anxious that we do not want to, in essence, humble ourselves before the Lord or others (1 Pet. 5:5)? I think pride is a response, a response to some latent or manifested fear . . . that people will not accord us the respect and dignity that we think we deserve if we humbled ourselves before the Lord or to them. It is that fear of being looked down upon, of being degraded, etc., which causes us to manifest pride and not be willing to humble ourselves. God says He will exalt us by His mighty hand if we humble ourselves to Him. That also means, where necessary, God will use men to exalt us and cause us to be exalted in the eyes of men.

When we are proud or display arrogance, it does not necessarily mean we are exalted, i.e. lifted up in the eyes of those around us that we 'intend' to notice. It often means we are exalted in our own eyes and minds. Pride does not evoke or necessitate a respect response. Exaltation does not happen when we are proud. It does not mean that people necessarily respect us more.

God, knowing these truths, therefore tells us to bring to Him all that makes us anxious and cast it at His feet, not on His shoulder because Jesus has borne the burden for us already and neither we nor He need to further bear anything. We also place them at His feet because Christ has placed all things under His feet and is seated in heavenly places, where He has placed all His and our enemies (including anxiety, fear, pride) under His feet (Eph. 1:20-23).

Therefore, let us also question ourselves what this pride might achieve next time . . . and really challenge ourselves to answer the question. What are we really anxious about? Why are we afraid of being humble in that circumstance? Remember, God exalts the humble and *resists* the proud (because fear and pride go hand in hand). Humility is actually the proof of faith that God will do what He says he will do when we are humble—i.e. to *exalt us*.

SET ON PURPOSE

Heb. 12:1-2, Col. 3:1-2

'SINCE THEN', 'THEREFORE', 'whereas', 'as it is now so', 'given that' . . . are all phrases to express the fact that a shift—a change—has taken place. Paul's admonishment therefore to us is that we should recognise that things are now different.

When summer officially translates into autumn in some parts of the world by the end of September, people set their watches differently and automatically adjust their lives to suit the new calendar. Paul is saying to us that we should set our minds on where Christ is, i.e. where we are also seated.

A clock that is set does not respond to what the old dictates. A clock set is a clock set. Set your minds in Christ and keep it set. A double-minded person cannot receive anything from the Lord (James 1:7-8). *Where are you currently seated, and what are the expectations of those who sit there?*

Set your mind to honour God and receive His blessings. Set your mind on the fact that summer is over and start wearing more (number of) clothes; change the setting of your heating thermostat.

Once your mind is set, the blessings will come your way. Setting your mind is somewhat like sowing and reaping. If your clock is set correctly, you will not go late to work.

Set your treasures (i.e. time, money, conversation, friendships, etc.) on Jesus and on heaven and your heart and mind will be there also—not to scrutinise them but to see them prosper.

It also works in a cyclically reinforcing manner. Just like in summer and winter, there is a putting on and a taking off some clothes and things. You cannot set your mind on Christ when your mind is still set on flesh. You cannot serve God and Mammon. You also cannot leave your mind blank after putting off evil things and desires. Indeed, the best way to change behaviour is to exchange behaviour.

'Since (therefore) you have been raised with Christ': (Col. 3:1-2) connotes that your faith is already set with Christ. This, therefore, is about actualising your thought life which Satan wars against daily (2 Cor. 10:4-6) and living life according to your faith. Set your TV channels; set what your read; set what you say.

FOR OUR OWN GOOD, SO WE MAY
SHARE IN HIS HOLINESS

My sons, do not make light of the Lord's discipline, and do not lose heart when the Lord rebukes you, because the Lord disciplines those whom He loves, and he punishes everyone he accepts as a son.

(Heb. 12:5-6)

WHEN YOU FIND a piece of precious stone, it is usually in the rough and requires some piece of work for the beauty and quality to be made apparent. When we go through this refining process or when our earthly fathers or bosses make us do this, it is usually as they best think—to serve their purpose. In Hebrews 12:10, the Bible tells us that God disciplines us for our own good.

God in His usual manner begins with the end in mind. Therefore, when we become God's children, what really happens is that we come into God's purpose for us, i.e. come to know about God's purpose for us. On God's part, that is when He begins to effectively connect with us to shape us into what He originally designed and predestined us for before the foundation of the world (Eph 1:4-6, 11). Therefore, God's chastisement or correction is actually preparatory work towards taking your place, making your mark, and fulfilling your purpose upon the earth—bringing Him glory.

To get to the place of your inheritance, there are things that God will have you correct today. It is when we do not heed or listen to God's voice that we get into problems later in life. To be sure, God's chastening is not just directly through the Holy Spirit telling us what we ought to do or not to do. It is also about God telling us through men, using our parents, family members, bosses, etc. to help us make those changes. The most painful correction I have come to know though is when I have refused to heed God's instruction and later had to change anyway because my future success at work, home, society, etc. demanded it. The challenge for us is in recognising which chastisement is coming from what source—whether from God or from men. Our Lord and Master learnt obedience by the things He suffered on earth.

TED THEODORE

ARE YOU MAKING RETURNS?

THE FOUR LEPERS were not just satisfied with thanking God and 'not believing' what great fortune had come to them (2 Kings 7:8-9). There is a time and a place for thanking God for all of His mercies, goodness, and favour . . . for bringing us out of bondage, sickness, poverty, ill reputation into a place of wealth, prominence, prestige, and honour. There is also a place to begin to use that God-given privilege, position, and power to bring in returns, as in fruits, to the kingdom.

Another big question or concern for me is whether I believe it is my right as a son to have these things, and if that is so, how have I used them? Do I act as if those are borrowed privileges that may pass away and I might well revert to my old state as a sick person, a poor, morally deficient person? Am I acting as though God might change His mind about His goodness and take my feet off the solid rock? Do I act in ways that are comparable in a sense to the servant who hid the talent? The real question is . . . for all the mercy, goodness, and favour the Lord has shown what is the return on our (kingdom) assets?

How much praise, testimony, and glory have returned to God because we are now His children with all these wonderful privileges? How many souls have been saved? How many people have rededicated their lives because they see in us the manifestation of the sons of God?

The twin challenge of not keeping our light under the bushel but letting it shine and the earth waiting for the manifestation of the sons of God should have us thinking differently as kings ourselves. This is not so much about not doing what we should not do. This is about doing what we should do. It is about being sure that we will use our assets rather than being concerned that we do not misuse our God-given assets. How have we used our God-given assets? Do we even act like it's ours? What different thing have we done lately for the kingdom in the way we use our assets? What qualifies us to dwell and enjoy kingdom benefits?

As we thank God for those mercies, wealth, etc., how many times have we used it for the glory of God apart from paying our tithes and offerings?

THE PREFACING QUESTION

Psalm 91

PSALM 91 PREFACES the protection of the Almighty by referencing how our positioning with the Lord (and His presence) does make a difference in the quantum and fullness of blessings that we receive from God. It starts thus: 'He who dwells in the secret place of the Most High shall abide/rest in the shadow of the Almighty'. Therefore, dwelling in that secret place and abiding in/under that shadow prefaces every other covenant blessing we may claim or lay claim to in the rest of Psalm 91. The real question therefore is . . . what does it take to abide/dwell under God's presence, sanctuary or shadow, and are we dwelling there?

Psalm 15:1 asks the same question and provides the answer in verse 2-5. These four verses set very clear criteria, making it clear what we need to do (to qualify) to abide, *not step in or pass through*, but to abide and dwell in God's sanctuary.

> Lord, who shall abide in thy tabernacle? who shall dwell in thy holy hill? He that walketh uprightly, and worketh righteousness, and speaketh the truth in his heart. He that backbiteth not with his tongue, nor doeth evil to his neighbour, nor taketh up a reproach against his neighbour. In whose eyes a vile person is contemned; but he honoureth them that fear the Lord. He that sweareth to his own hurt, and changeth not. He that putteth not out his money to usury, nor taketh reward against the innocent. He that doeth these things shall never be moved. (Ps. 15:1-5)

As it were, God has set His standards, and as is with Him, the choice is ours. What brings it home to me is how we all have our core values, and based on our core values, we choose those people we want to be close to us or not. Thus, based on our core values, we might extend ourselves, our love, protection, etc. to others who may not be so close to us—the natural benefactors of our inheritance. What drives us to and from people (if we have a choice) is how aligned they are with our core values. How aligned are we to God's core values and, therefore, are full beneficiaries of His fullness and goodness?

Psalm 15:2-5 is very important because the manifestation of Psalm 91:2-16 is very much dependent on Psalm 15:2-4, except where mercy comes in.

How qualified are you? Will your life attract God's presence? Will your speech, the use of your tongue, qualify you or not? How do you treat your neighbour?

ARE YOU READY AND MINDFUL?

2 Samuel 18

And David numbered the people that were with him, and set captains of thousands, and captains of hundreds over them. And David sent forth a third part of the people under the hand of Joab, and a third part under the hand of Abishai the son of Zeruiah, Joab's brother, and a third part under the hand of Ittai the Gittite. And the king said unto the people, I will surely go forth with you myself also. But the people answered, Thou shalt not go forth: for if we flee away, they will not care for us; neither if half of us die, will they care for us: but now thou art worth ten thousand of us: therefore now it is better that thou succour us out of the city. And the king said unto them, What seemeth you best I will do. And the king stood by the gate side, and all the people came out by hundreds and by thousands. And the king commanded Joab and Abishai and Ittai, saying, Deal gently for my sake with the young man, even with Absalom. And all the people heard when the king gave all the captains charge concerning Absalom (2 Sam. 18:1-5).

For the battle was there scattered over the face of all the country: and the wood devoured more people that day than the sword devoured. And Absalom met the servants of David. And Absalom rode upon a mule, and the mule went under the thick boughs of a great oak, and his head caught hold of the oak, and he was taken up between the heaven and the earth; and the mule that was under him went away (2 Sam. 18:8-9).

ABSALOM WAS AT war with his father David, and chapter 18 starts with a description of what seemed to be a momentous and important battle in this war. Given the conversations between David and his commanders, this battle seemed quite epic and decisive, too important for David to be out at battle on this occasion. Absalom's situation however seemed to be different, and that is the focus of this inquiry—to search out truths that we could use for ourselves even today. A couple of questions . . .

- Why was Absalom riding alone without any guards at this time?
- Why did his advisers and commanders not advise him as David's had?
- Who were his advisers? And who are yours today?
- Why was he not ready for battle? This was a time of battle/war and he had no sword on him, thus could not cut himself loose. Are you battle ready? Ready to draw your sword, i.e. speak God's Word for that specific occasion.
- He was riding a mule in a battle, not a horse. Is your horse prepared for battle?
- Did he quite realise the season and territory he was in? Otherwise, why would he be riding a mule, alone, without a sword in a time of war when the forest was claiming more people then swords? What season and context are you playing in today?
- Who is on your side? Who are you listening to? Are you even listening to your advisers, counsellors . . . ? Who says Absalom had no access to counsel?

Thy testimonies also are my delight and my counsellors.
(Ps. 119:24)

TED THEODORE

YOU DO NOT NEED ONE MORE MAN

Judges 7

A COMBINED ARMY of 135,000 troops, armed with swords and war paraphernalia, besieged Gideon. All he had with him was an army of 30,000 men. This was already daunting enough for Gideon, who was still in early days (in his walk with God and in leading Israel to battles). He had never really gone into battle, let alone led one. Indeed, he was just coming out of a fleece test with God, trying to determine if God indeed was true to His Word. So here was someone, like some of us today, who was yet struggling with unbelief, yet God chose him to lead Israel into battle.

This is quite pertinent to God and us today, giving us a vision of what He wants us to achieve despite our inadequacies and inabilities. In verse 2, before they stepped out for battle, the *Lord* said to Gideon, 'The people that are with thee are too many for me to give the Midianites into their hands, lest Israel vaunt themselves against me, saying, "Mine own hand hath saved me."' The test for reducing the number of men with Gideon (please note men, not armies) by about 70 per cent to 10,000 men was to separate those with or without fear. God could have delivered their enemies into their hands even with 70 per cent fearful men, but God first of all works by faith not fear. About 70 per cent of those men manifested fear, and God is telling us through this story that fear will always limit the impact of faith in His plans for us. He is able to use us as He wants to if we do not allow fear to inhabit us and if we do not look unto ourselves, our wisdom, our knowledge, our societal background, etc. to justify what we are able or not to accomplish. Do not go by what you see, neither let the things you see or hear create fear in your heart because God wants to do greater things despite what we think of ourselves and what we think we are qualified for.

Eventually, God saved them with 300 men—a ratio of 1:450 soldiers, and this proves to us that we do not need more years of experience, more money, and more clout to be used by God. You do not need one more (fearful) man; all you need is to be available for God to use, to declare His glory, and to acknowledge *Him*! You do not need one more man!

THE GRACE OF PURPOSE

PURPOSE IS THE key. Purpose is primary. Purpose propels. Without purpose, achievement and accomplishment would have no context. As we go through life, as we live out our desires and purpose, we sometimes would go through situations that may distract us or detract from us, fully accomplishing our purpose.

A purpose is that which also keeps us steady in the race when we have victory and/or are going through the challenges of life. Isaac, one of the unsung heroes and Bible personalities, was a man of purpose. Not just a man of purpose, he also knew what his purpose was.

His name, Isaac, meant laughter, and laughter in a joyful sense, not in a mocking sense. He was meant to bring joy and hope to his family. However, the same name that seemed to be a blessing later become an object of scorn and derision by his half-brother. Isaac had to live with this scorn until his mother insisted that Ishmael leave the house. And just as Isaac was getting to settle in as the sole heir in his father's house, there was another *inflection—his father was going to offer him as a sacrifice.*

Let me talk about inflections for a while. Inflections are events in your life, positive and otherwise, which have the potential to derail you from your purpose. It could range from a promotion to a temptation, from overflow to sudden lack, from a point of strength to a point of weakness. One point about inflection is that it has the potential to deflect us towards or from our purpose.

WHAT YOU ARE HOLDING MAY
BE HOLDING ON TO YOU

Acts: 10:4-16, Ecclesiastes 3:1

FOR EVERY TIME God gives us a specific word, there is a purpose for that word and a season for that word. God's Word is for all times and all seasons and is applicable to all of His children. However, He deals with each of us as individuals based on the purpose we are meant to achieve or based on what we are going through at that time of life. For example, the law says you should drive with your car license plate being quite visible always. However, on your wedding date, in some countries it is okay to drive with 'Just Married'; on any other day, you may pay quite some fine.

What you have today may be very attractive. However, what you have today may not be suited or suitable for where you are headed. You should dress up for wherever you are headed. Joseph dressed up for the palace though he was yet in the prison, even though he could have waited to get to the palace before changing his clothes. Maybe that would have been too late. Whenever you are looking at the next level in life, you should start behaving or dressing like people at that next stage of life. It may be very difficult though to leave behind the attire we are currently wearing because of the great experiences we had in that particular attire because of whatever compliments people gave us when we were wearing that attire. Letting go can be very difficult. Parents are for a purpose and time; there is a time for children to move on, and thereafter you can still support them—though the relationship changes.

What you hold so dearly today might be what you need to lose to move forward into the next phase of your life. Abraham had to move away from Lot and Haran to get to his land of promise. The Israelites had to let go of leek, cucumber, and garlic and the memory of all of Egypt to get into the Promised Land. They almost lost the promise of the Promised Land because of their inability to let go of Egypt from their minds. In Acts 10:4-16, God was about to elevate Peter's ministry as the avenue for bringing Gentile sons to glory into God's kingdom. Peter almost lost the opportunity as he was holding on to traditions that had served well in the past.

What made you successful up to this point in your life may not be able to take you further; otherwise it would have taken you further. Elijah had the ravens to feed him for a short while and the widow woman to sustain him for a longer time.

Do not turn an experience into a doctrine or a philosophy. It does not matter how great that experience was, e.g. the experience at the mount of transfiguration, Jacob at Bethel—where angels were ascending and descending. He could have stayed there and made more out of it than there really was. This is not in any way to despise what happened in Bethel, but there were greater things in Jacob's future—just like yours.

Solomon moved from money to wisdom, to worship . . . to women—in the wrong direction.

Except the seed of a thing dies, it abides alone. Therefore, you may need to sow that experience, sow that pride, and sow that accomplishment and see your growth and your future. 'He that loveth his life shall lose it; and he that hateth his life in this world shall keep it unto life eternal'—(John 12:25).

> The king's heart is like a stream . . . Is God ordering your stream?
>
> (Prov. 21:1)

PAY YOUR VOWS TO THE LORD

But I will sacrifice unto thee with the voice of thanksgiving; I will pay that that I have vowed. Salvation is of the LORD.

(Jon. 2:9)

'Your word, whatever you say, is very important to God and to the devil!' God told the Israelites.

As truly as I live, saith the LORD, as ye have spoken in mine ears, so will I do to you.

(Num. 14:28)

IT IS BAD enough to think ungodly thoughts, for out of the fullness, abundance of the heart, a man speaks. It makes things worse when you then actually give life to those words by voicing them out.

Your words are important, and that's also why in Numbers 30, Moses lays out principles concerning vows. God is not impressed by the goodness of our vows and intentions, so do not let situations or pressures get you to say things you do not mean or intend to fulfil (Eccles. 5:1-7).

Ananias and Sapphira died because of the gap between their vows and their actions; they did not fulfil their vows (Acts 5).

Often it is not so much about God being angry; it is also about the devil accusing the saints before God. For example, when you say you are a man of integrity and your child says in front of a neighbour's child that he will give his bicycle to a child in the neighbourhood or to his sister after he receives his new bike and does not do it. Would you still buy the new bike for him so that he retains both? What would be your response to the neighbour's child if he complains to you that your son is not fulfilling his vows, which you observed? What would you also say to your son?

DO NOT SERVE GOD ON YOUR OWN
SECULAR OR SPIRITUAL TERMS

But it displeased Jonah exceedingly, and he was very angry.

(Jonah 4:1)

SERVICE MEANS SOMEONE is receiving something from you; therefore, whatever you are doing ought to be motivated by the interest of that person. John 3:30 says, 'He must increase and I must decrease', in reference to our response to the will of God and our service unto God.

In the Lord's prayer, we say, 'Let thy will be done . . .' Jonah wanted to serve God but had his own ideas about what should happen—about how the Lord should answer his prayers. When we serve God, He will do more than we can think or ask!

Peter had same struggles with accepting to pray for Cornelius, but he did only out of obedience to God.

Jesus only did what pleased God because He did what He saw His father do.

'Working for' and 'walking with' are two different experiences—Judas worked for and Peter/John walked with.

God is merciful and honours our repentance (Jon. 4:2).

He forgave Peter who repented—Judas did not repent . . .

He forgave Nineveh and Jonah.

He forgives even your impromptu promises, declarations, and vows, so confess and repent of them today as soon as you realise you're on the wrong path.

RIGHTEOUSNESS PREPARES THE WAY

Righteousness shall go before him; and shall set us in the way of his steps.

(Ps. 85:13)

THE PSALMIST HERE was concerned about restoration with God—about restoration of his position and place with God. This is evident from the first two verses and continues through this chapter.

When often I hear the word *restoration* being used, it of course connotes to me a change for the better in the fortune and situation of that person. And yes, it is so! It could also be seen quite differently in the sense of preparatory activities that make it possible to restore. The very idea of restoration means that there are two stories involved—both may be yours or not, but at least one should be yours at the end of the process. Thus, the word 'restore' may have broader applications other than bringing back to new. It may, as in this study, mean bringing to a new bigger, better place. The idea here is that restoration may be akin to repackaging.

If God is the one who restores, whether it is bringing back to the old form or repackaging us in the sense of restoring us, then at some point in our lives there is a trigger that causes God to act. Verse 13 says that righteousness goes before God's presence and prepares the way for the steps of God. What this means is that if we begin to lead and live righteously, then we will be preparing the way for Him to step into our situation because God is never far away from righteousness.

Therefore, we do not need to be run-down before God shows up. Also God does not just show up. He shows up where there is righteousness. Righteousness and peace go hand in hand. Peace is another prerequisite. 'Righteousness looks down from heaven' (Ps. 85:11); God is never far away from righteousness.

God stepped into Sodom to redeem and restore Lot—righteousness attracts God.

In Psalm 85:9 we see that God, His salvation, and His glory are all intertwined. God is near to those who fear Him (those who live in righteousness). We can prepare for our restoration to glory, for our salvation, by living righteously, and God is never far behind.

John the Baptist lived righteously and Jesus showed up.
Joseph lived righteously and was restored from Potiphar's house.

God is never far away from the righteous indeed He is seeking them.

(2 Chr. 16:9)

YOUR ENEMIES HAVE NO CHOICE

When a man's ways are pleasing to the *LORD*, He makes even his enemies to live at peace with him.

(Prov. 16:7)

WHAT REALLY STRIKES me here is that God makes our enemies to be at peace; it is not like they want to be at peace by themselves. Your enemies will not just wake up and desire to be at peace with you. This is because it is not in their character to do so—the devil is wicked and mean.

Jehoshaphat was a man and a king whose heart was devoted to God—to the ways of God.

And his heart was lifted up in the ways of the *LORD*.

(2 Chron. 17:6)

The Bible records that he sent officials round Israel to teach the people the Word of the Lord. As he did this: 'The fear of the Lord fell on all the kingdoms of the lands surrounding Judah, so that they did not make war against Jehoshaphat' (*note against Jehoshaphat, not Israel*).

And the fear of the *LORD* fell upon all the kingdoms of the lands that were round about Judah, so that they made no war against Jehoshaphat.

(2 Chron. 17:10)

The fear of the Lord (and His presence) comes upon your enemies as you serve Him.

Your enemies will not only stop intimidating you; they will bring gifts to make peace with you—*only* because your ways are pleasing to God. Like in Psalm 91:14, the Lord promises to protect us because we love Him. He will rescue us because we acknowledge His name.

Like the eagle that flies directly towards the direct glare of the sun when threatened, so should we be as Christians. When we notice our enemies not being at peace with us, like the eagle, we should fly and move closer towards God. The reason the other prey birds give up chasing the eagle is that they cannot look directly into the rays of the sun. Also, when we walk in the ways of God, His presence is ever near, and His presence will chase away every evil presence. If your enemies are gaining an upper hand and are not in fact seeking peace with you, then you should move closer to the sun and God will *make* them be at peace with you. Laban had no choice in Genesis 31:24 when God told him, 'Take heed that thou speak not to Jacob either good or bad'. Nothing! That was the favour of peace that was upon Jacob.

> God is looking to show Himself strong on the behalf of those whose hearts are perfect towards him.
>
> (2 Chron. 16:9)

DON'T SEND A BOY TO DO A MAN'S JOB

*Turning to Jether, his oldest son, he said, 'Kill them!' But Jether did
not draw his sword, because he was only a boy and was afraid.*

(Judg. 8:20)

GIDEON WAS A cowering, cowardly man before the *Lord* met him,
hiding away from the Midianites (threshing wheat in a wine press).
It was the grace and power of God that made him into a mighty man of
valour and gave him the confidence to do all the things that needed doing,
to fulfil the purpose of God. Gideon had a key role in God's purpose and
plan to deliver the Israelites from the clutches of the Midianites who had
oppressed them for so long. It was in this pursuit that he went after Zebah
and Zalmunna, the kings of Midian.

After a long and arduous battle, Gideon and his son, Jether, finally caught
them. Gideon then asked his son to draw his *sword* and kill them, but his
son did not because he was too young and was afraid. There are a couple of
lessons worth looking into here.

Firstly, it is clear that this boy was young. Though he was young, he
was the eldest child of Gideon, the man of valour. The point here is that
the fact that he was the eldest son does not automatically mean that he was
going to be a warrior or a man of valour like his father. Too often we forget
the grace of purpose and that it is the grace that enables us to accomplish
certain things as individuals that other (more capable) people cannot achieve.
Grace and purpose, i.e. God's purpose, can often not be transferred from one
person to the other, even as a result of physical closeness. God gives to every
man as He wills. Gideon obviously was not operating in these dimensions
because he probably thought that the anointing and grace to be a man of
valour was easily transferable.

The second point to note, related to the first, is that Jether, Gideon's
youngest son, was with him, at least for a part of this pursuit. Jether also
had a *sword*. What it would seem like for Jether was that though he had

seen battle with his eyes, it looked as though he had not *experienced* battle. He was with his father, but his father had not spent any time training him or breaking him into the act and discipline of warfare. It is important that before we ask people to handle crucial and very important tasks we prepare them or get a sense of what they are able to accomplish. At the least, they should have a sense of self-worth or some experience they can reference the current tasks to. David, when he had to face Goliath, referenced God's grace when he killed the lion and the bear bare-handed. Jether obviously had not done anything like this previously, and when the stakes were raised, he could not perform because he had neither grace nor experience. If you desire your child or anybody to be able to do something in some capacity when they grow up, then you should first seek to understand their purpose and the grace that is upon their lives and therein prepare them. Imagine the risk that Gideon would have taken if he had left the kings to the hands of Jether without being present. His months of pursuit would have been vain.

The third lesson here is that Jether did not kill because he was afraid. Fear cripples. Fear binds. It was not only that he was young; he was afraid and probably was scared of the kings and their regalia/apparel and could not rise to the occasion. Often in life, what stops us from achieving more is doing something that we are not sure of or doing anything that we are scared of. Though Jether was young, he could have killed them had he not been afraid. God's grace that was upon his father, Gideon, was not upon him. Gideon was also scared, but became bold after the Word of the Lord came upon him in Judges 6:12. You need God's Word to liberate you from fear—to give you freedom to act. This was part of Jesus purpose here on earth (Luke 4:18).

What makes you a man is not age, nor worldly wisdom. What makes us men in every situation is the Word of God upon our situation, upon our lives. It was the Word that turned Peter from shivering flax into the great apostle of the early church. It was God's Word that moved Moses back to Egypt from the wilderness and that turned the disciples from illiterate fishermen to ministers, and very bold ones at that.

Chronologically, being a boy or man does not mean so much when God's Word is in force. This is reinforced in Job 32:6-9: 'And Elihu the son of Barachel the Buzite answered and said, "I am young, and ye are very old; wherefore I was afraid, and durst not shew you mine opinion."[7] I said, "Days should speak, and multitude of years should teach wisdom. But there is a spirit in man: and the inspiration of the Almighty giveth them understanding."

Elihu was afraid also (Job 32:6), and it was the spirit of God (Job 32:8) that broke it! It is the spirit of God in man that gives understanding, not the spirit of fear. Before you take on a task, be sure you have the wisdom, the anointing, and grace of God upon you, for that is what makes you a man—ready to use the sword.

THERE'S MORE THAN THE EYES CAN SEE . . .

> Gideon and his three hundred men, exhausted yet keeping up the pursuit, came to the Jordan and crossed it. He said to the men of Succoth, 'Give my troops some bread; they are worn out, and I am still pursuing Zebah and Zalmunna, the kings of Midian.' But the officials of Succoth said, 'Do you already have the hands of Zebah and Zalmunna in your possession? Why should we give bread to your troops?'
>
> (Judg. 8:4-6)

GIDEON WAS IN pursuit of the kings of Midian with his 300 troops and had been at that for a while, chasing them through several towns. It was during his pursuit that he passed through Succoth. At that point, his men were very tired and needed to refresh themselves before going on. The officials of Succoth declined his request on the grounds that he did not yet have the kings in captivity. *This sort of rejection is fairly typical of what we see from men who look at what we have and are today and make decisions about us rather than look at the potential we hold.*

Do not judge people by what you see with your physical eyes. The men of Succoth must have been looking at the 300 ragged than usual men. The people of Succoth were more interested in relating with them if they had something to offer.

Sow seeds and do not look on the natural when you sow, also do not sow where you are expecting to be paid back (*note that this is different from where you hope to receive*). One reason the officials of Succoth and Penuel were killed was that they refused to sow because they could not be instantly guaranteed of results/returns. In fact, they were not really willing to sow; what they wanted to do was to exchange favours. This is very different from sowing; that is why Jesus said that unless a seed does, it abides alone. They were unwilling for their seeds to die and produce a bounty. How do you give and to whom do you give? What determines who you respond to in times of need? Do you give if you have a certainty that the recipient of a favour—like the men of Succoth and Penuel—would repay? This kind of sowing is not acting in faith and anything that is not from faith cannot and does not please God (Heb. 11:6).

The men of Succoth and Penuel did not recognise the grace and gift of God upon Gideon. They could not sense the new anointing that was upon the life of Gideon, even when there were very obvious signs. They were so blinded by their preconceptions and prejudices that they could not see God at work in 300 untrained men who were sacking all of their enemies.

LOOK FOR THE SEED, NOT THE FINISHED PRODUCT

And the princes of Succoth said, 'Are the hands of Zebah and Zalmunna now in thine hand, that we should give bread unto thine army?' And Gideon said, 'Therefore when the *LORD* hath delivered Zebah and Zalmunna into mine hand, then I will tear your flesh with the thorns of the wilderness and with briers.' And he went up thence to Penuel, and spake unto them likewise: and the men of Penuel answered him as the men of Succoth had answered him.

(Judg. 8:6-8)

THE SEEDS OF greatness were all evident in Gideon, but the men of Succoth and Penuel were looking for fruits. In all of God's creation and dealings with men, what He looks for and works with is seed. Gideon's call, Moses, etc. were all as seeds. Jesus came as a seed. This is why God looks at the heart and not the external, and if we would reap some reward and obtain God's righteousness and harvest, then we must think *seed*. When you look at a female for a wife, look for the seed of what you want, not the fruit per se. What to pay attention to when investing is the potential to deliver. If these kings had been looking at the potential that Gideon (with God's promise and grace upon his life) had, they would have responded otherwise.

Believe in people and in their abilities. *When you believe in people and you actualise this by trusting them, what you are doing in effect is that you are sowing to their future.* You are responding to their potential, and you will get back from them what otherwise may not have been feasible.

Let the love of God guide you in your response to people. Those men were hungry. Those men were their brothers, i.e. fellow Israelites who were acting for God, not to mention that they were seen fighting for everyone's deliverance. Love should have motivated them to give or to respond. What they rather did was judge the people, looking at how they were dressed. Let us rather act or respond in love.

Finally, respond to seed, give in love, expect in faith, and God will bless you.

PURPOSEFUL COMMUNICATION

Let no corrupt communication proceed out of your mouth, but that which is good to the use of edifying, that it may minister grace unto the hearers.

(Eph. 4:29)

WHEN PAUL TALKS here about unwholesome talk or conversation, he is referring to a conversation that does not meet the purpose of benefiting those who listen. Paul, in effect, was setting a new standard, a litmus test for the efficiency and value of our conversations.

Subjected to more scrutiny, the question really is whether our conversations are borne out of love for the recipient or not. When we have something to say, do we truly ask ourselves if and how this would make a difference to the hearer/listener? Love should make us look out for the other's interest, more than just our interests.

Love, inspiring our conversations, will make us listen more to others so that we can adequately respond to their needs. Listening becomes more than just an act: It shows up as respect for the other person. It becomes a means to help us provide service or respond adequately to the listener. So we listen (and respond) in love.

To avoid unwholesome talk means that we need to judge what we want to say before we say it. Talk is unwholesome when it does not build up others according to their needs, based on the Word of God. Their needs in this case could be time related. This means that what is needful today may not be what's needful tomorrow. We therefore need to rely on the Holy Ghost to teach us what to say at every point of our life as we communicate with others. I use communicate here because it includes emails, letters, text messages, etc.

The judge of how well we have communicated or not is the receiver and the love of God. With all good intentions, if it does not benefit the listener, then the communication/message is meaningless from a love point of view.

Always begin with the end in mind. In this sense, conversations become a point of sowing into the lives of others. Conversations will be about giving, not telling; enriching, not stripping others' self-esteem. It is about building up others. As we sow in love, we also will receive in love. Amen!

REJOICE!

O VER THE COURSE of Paul's life, he made a choice to rejoice in spite of the situations around him, despite all the hardship around and the unpleasantness thereof.

a) To rejoice or not is a choice. Paul says explicitly, 'Rejoice in the Lord always and again I say rejoice' (Phil. 4:4).

We should rejoice because the joy of the Lord is our strength (Neh. 8:10). Without strength, we cannot fight, nor even attempt to. The enemy knows that without joy you simply have no chance. That is why in Philippians 4:5, Paul says, 'Let your moderation be known to all men . . .', not just to you.

b) The reason for rejoicing was the prayers that were being offered and the help of the Holy Spirit. Paul was always praying for others and was confident that his prayers were being answered. This is why he said in Philippians 4:6, 'Be careful for nothing; but in everything by prayer and supplication with thanksgiving let your requests be made known unto God'. Prayers said in faith lead us to rejoice in advance of the answers—rejoicing creates the expectation and hope—which causes the Holy Spirit to work on our behalf.

The help of the Holy Spirit in his role as a comforter makes rejoicing possible. Call on Him to cultivate a relationship and conversational pattern with Him. Lay your burdens on Him. Care for nothing (Phil. 4:6). With your burdens, you cannot rejoice. Rejoicing brings peace. 'And the peace of God, which passeth all understanding, shall keep your hearts and minds through Christ Jesus' (Phil. 4:7).

c) Eagerly expect and hope that you will not be ashamed. The Bible says the expectation of the righteous shall not be cut off (Prov. 23:18, 24:14) and that hope maketh not ashamed (Rom. 5:5). Let your rejoicing be fuelled by your expectation. Rejoice knowing that God is causing all things to work together for our good (Rom. 8:28).

d) You need courage to go through. Courage comes because you know you will not be ashamed and are sure of a positive end result. It is courage borne out of faith in answered prayers and the comfort of the Holy Spirit which makes us rejoice.

ATTRACTING DIVINE ATTENTION

And Noah builded an altar unto the *LORD;* and took of every clean beast, and of every clean fowl, and offered burnt offerings on the altar.

(Gen. 8:20)

And God blessed Noah and his sons, and said unto them, Be fruitful, and multiply, and replenish the earth. And the fear of you and the dread of you shall be upon every beast of the earth, and upon every fowl of the air, upon all that moveth upon the earth, and upon all the fishes of the sea; into your hand are they delivered.

(Gen. 9:1-2)

GOD HONOURS SACRIFICE. Several times in the Bible, this is confirmed in several ways both in the Old and New Testaments. This is partly so because sacrifice always involves giving and in this case giving unto God.

In essence a sacrifice (whether of money, time, or any other resource) involves a couple of things:

a) Depriving yourself of something important to you. It has to be something that has an opportunity cost to it, and generally the higher the personal attachment, the higher the cost, the greater the sacrifice and the blessings thereof. *You should not expect to trap/catch a buffalo with lizard bait! A deer would make more inviting bait, I'd think!*

b) A sacrifice also often connotes sowing into the life of someone else, and in the cases we are looking at here, it actually involves sowing into God; and God honours sacrifice. Because we sow unto God, it makes it special.

c) Sacrifice unto God should be inspired by the acknowledgement that God is greater than whatever the alternative use of that thing or time is. The sacrifice is incomparable in worth to God, and that should inspire us; for example, when we sacrifice time we should have spent with TV or a friend (consciously) to read God's Word, God honours it.

d) God responds to all forms of sacrifice, especially material sacrifice. Why material? My response firstly will be to ask, 'Why does material giving bother you the most?' That is the same reason it is important to God because it is important to you, and God knows what 'pain' we feel when we truly sacrifice or offer things in sacrifice. God is 'attracted' by the *love that propels the extent of self-deprivation*, not so much by simply the size of the offering. In Psalm 51:17, God requires a broken spirit and a contrite and broken heart. This is important because a broken spirit and a broken heart recognise that something is greater than it. After all, only the stronger can break the less strong. 'He must increase, but I must decrease' (John 3:30). Only a broken spirit can submit to and reverence God.

The effect of a material gift can break your heart and spirit, but so can the fulfilment of the promise change your life.

God responded to Abel, Noah, Abraham, Jacob, Solomon, David, Jesus, and Cornelius when they sacrificed (material gifts) to God.

CURRENCY NOT STATUS

Paul was writing and at same time instructing Timothy on the virtues of a minister in both letters to Timothy. In the first letter to Timothy, in Chapter 4, verse 9-10, Paul says, 'This is a faithful saying and worthy of all acceptation. For therefore we both labour and suffer reproach, because we trust in the living God, who is the Saviour of all men, specially of those that *believe*.'

(1 Tim. 4:9)

BELIEVING OR TO be termed a believer is not a status. It is a reference to the condition of your faith in the Word and person of Jesus Christ at any given point in time.

That you are a believer, i.e. born again, having accepted at some *milestone* day in your life the Lordship of Jesus Christ, does not make you powerful, regardless of what you currently are doing. We should put that hope in God and expect Him to be our saviour (in times of need).

God responds to the currency of your faith, not necessary your status. In fact, the currency of your faith and standing with God actually affects the amount of hope we put in God (and His ability to respond to us in times of need).

In Hebrews 4:14-16, the Bible talks about us holding firmly to the faith we profess '. . . so that we can confidently approach the throne of grace in our time of need'. What gives us the confidence is that we are holding fast, not that we held fast sometime ago or are known as those who held fast sometime ago. The real question is, 'Are you holding fast to faith in God's plan for your need today?'

What this means is that when we are faced with a situation, what is important is not simply that we are believers (as a status). What is rather important is that we believe a specific word to work on our behalf in that situation. It's like the Bible says in 2 Chronicles 16:9, 'The eyes of the Lord goeth to and fro the earth seeking to show Himself strong on the behalf of those whose hearts are perfect towards Him'. What the Lord is seeking during these visits is the *now* faith. The currency of faith He can work with—those whose hearts are *now* perfect towards Him.

It is the 'currency' of the unbeliever that gets attention from the Holy Spirit and gets born again, not because of their status. When they make that life choice to believe that Jesus is the Christ and decide to put their hope in Him, then the Holy Spirit shows up and ministers salvation to them

Here's the sequence the way I see it.

'I believe . . . therefore I have hope' (in that specific word that *I believe*). I have currency of belief (not status). God often steps in as a saviour, especially of those who believe (in a specific word) not those who are generic believers.

Thus, the Bible says, 'I believe, therefore I speak'. It is easy to tell the currency of your belief just by listening to you in a short time. What are you saying/professing today about your situation—'I believed, therefore have I spoken . . .' (Ps. 116:10)?

'I know in whom I (have) believe (d) and He is able . . .' We believe in God, and God and His words are inseparable. So when we quote that verse (2 Tim. 1:12), we are inevitably saying that we know the Word of God on which we are standing. When Paul says in 2 Timothy 1:12 that 'I am convinced that he is able to guard what I have entrusted to him for that day', he is really saying I have entrusted my belief in God, that there is a Word of God that I believe and have entrusted my hope in God.

Our currency, our language, and our communication need to remain valid and relevant to tap into the faithfulness of God. In 2 Timothy 2:13, Paul reminds us, 'If we are faithless, he will remain faithful, for he cannot disown himself'. What this means in a sense is that we cannot afford to act and speak faithlessness because God is not going to change His currency of faith just so He can save us. Yes, there is grace and mercy, and we should yet know that; however, the currency of our faith is key in determining God's response to us.

So that verse of scripture is really saying that God will remain faithful to Himself and His Word, not merely being faithful to our unfaithfulness or faithfulness.

TED THEODORE

HE IS ABLE TO DO . . . ABOVE

Now unto him that is able to do exceeding abundantly above all that we ask or think, according to the power that worketh in us. Unto him be glory in the church by Christ Jesus throughout all ages, world without end. Amen.

(Eph. 3:20)

PAUL EXPOUNDS ON the nature of our Father, our God. God is able—this is a measure of His ability, of His immeasurable wisdom and strength. In John 1:1, we learn there was nothing that was made that was made without Him. All life, all creation, originally consisted and emanated from Him.

God is able to do exceeding. The term *exceed* means 'over', 'beyond', 'across', 'superior to'. God is able to go beyond what we expect to give us something else (instead of) because of His abilities. This is why we should thank Him in all things and all ways.

God is able to do exceeding abundantly. God is able to do far beyond that which we ask for.

We need to start from a point of view that we do not often quite know (in all humility) what we want. For example, if we want a car or a house, we can describe a couple of features we believe are important, but often forget a couple of other important things; for example, did you remember to ask about a spouse who will not think it's okay to pick their nose in public?

We need to know that God is not only able, but He is also willing—that is why He sent His Son. There is a power at work in us; there are riches that we have inherited.

The eyes of your understanding being enlightened; that ye may know what is the hope of his calling, and what the riches of the glory of his inheritance in the saints, And what is the exceeding greatness of his power to us-ward who believe, according to the working of his mighty power.

(Eph. 1:18-19)

This is why God is keen for us to succeed. He is also keen because He loves us.

We need to continually give Him glory, for in simple things God is really at the core of our lives. He gives us children and wisdom; gives us promotion, health, favour; and shields us from evil. Let us thank Him!

TED THEODORE

THE VIRTUES OF STEWARDSHIP

Matthew 25:14-30

STEWARDSHIP REQUIRES THE steward to acknowledge what they have been entrusted with in the true sense. What this means is that the steward must see the task, role, and/or opportunity as their *own* for the period of time they are entrusted with it.

There are really two reinforcing points.

Firstly, the steward should 'own' their roles as their own. To own that role as theirs, they would have to trust their benefactor that these benefactors are truly releasing the opportunity or authority to them so that they can operate in that space as their own.

The converse of this is that where there is no trust (by the steward), that he has been empowered, the steward would not 'own' the role or task and therefore would not put in their best into the role.

A crucial assumption of this trust and ownership cycle is that the steward needs to be clear (by asking) about what they are responsible for in that relationship; for example, what are the boundaries for responsibility and accountability. As a steward, you need to be clear without making assumptions like the hired steward in this story. Clarify your thoughts and intentions with your benefactors—even where there is trust, to solidify that trust.

Once all that is settled, the steward needs to put in a decent day's job for a decent day's pay. Strive to leave the task better than it was when you got it. Strive to make a difference—with joy in your heart.

The reward of stewardship transcends the challenge of more responsibilities. It also involves sharing in the master's happiness. Imagine what God will do when He is happy . . . when you do something that pleases Him! If we truly work unto the Lord, then we'll be getting the Lord's reward, not our earthly master's. The biggest reward is sharing in the joy of the Lord.

READINESS

Mark 2:18-22

IN MARK 2:18-22, Jesus tells the story of putting new wine into old wineskins and putting a new cloth patch on to an old tear. While it does sound stupid that anyone should put new wine with all its vigour and sparkle into an old wineskin, which cannot hold it, the point here is really about containment and the readiness to receive.

There are key things that God wants to deal with us about so that we are ready to receive the blessings He has in store for us. Until we are ready to receive, i.e. prepared and ready, we would not be able to receive the fullness of God.

Transforming from the old wineskin to a new skin is the process of being born again. Where we first become born again, we move from a state of not being able to communicate and receive God's spirit to a state where God can relate and can pour Himself into us. That, however, is just the first step.

Being able to receive is also like the pitcher or goalkeeper who is ready to throw a ball and needs to be sure that the catcher or attacker is ready to receive it. In fact, sometimes the one who has the ball signals to the fellow player to receive before throwing the ball, just to be sure that the receiver frees himself from the opponents. This is akin to freeing ourselves from the things of this world that tend to hold us down. We need to rid ourselves of those encumbrances and those sins that beset us, e.g. hobbies, passion, plans. Then we truly can make room for God's full spiritual manifestation—the real thing.

Compare this to overeating. When we overeat, at least when I do, it is almost like being drunk as my spirit becomes close to numb. That is why fasting puts us in a place of readiness to hear from God. It is not just the act of fasting itself but the absence of other things that could clutter our minds which makes the difference.

The real question is that now that we are born again . . . are we able to receive God's spirit and respond—being new wine vessels ready for every new outpouring?

ABRAHAM, PATTERNS

- Terah was headed for Canaan but stopped at Haran.
- God called Abraham to go to Canaan, and he took Lot along.
- Lot, Terah's grandson, wanted to stay, in fact stayed at Sodom and Gomorrah.
- Was there something about not finishing the course here between Terah and Lot that Abraham had to break?

Is there something—a pattern—that you need to break in your life?

LIFTING UP (HOLY) HANDS

Exodus 17:9-15

THE ISRAELITES WERE at war with the Amalekites, and Moses was leading them in this battle. It was a battle that the Lord commissioned (verse 14). When they were in battle, as long as Moses raised up his hands, they had the victory, and when his hands grew weary and he dropped them, they would be losing.

Lifting up hands unto heaven, in this case lifting up of the staff of authority in his hands, was essentially recognising the supremacy, the victory of God over the affairs of men. When we lift up our hands in praise and in deference to God, we are essentially saying that God has the final say in our lives and that our contact with Him is more important than whatever it is we are facing.

> Behold, bless ye the LORD, all ye servants of the LORD, which by night stand in the house of the LORD. Lift up your hands in the sanctuary, and bless the LORD.
>
> (Ps. 134:1-2)

In this verse and in various other verses of the Bible, lifting up of our hands is synonymous with praising God, giving God glory and adoration. What this battle with the Amalekites teaches us is that as long as we praise God, giving Him the glory, as long as we lift up holy hands to God, we would always be victorious.

The battle is important, but the praise is more important. The battle looks real, but it's praise, the lifting up of holy hands that controls the battle. In 1 Timothy 2:8, Paul admonished the men to lift up holy hands in prayer without anger or disputing. The added emphasis here is that we should not dispute, quarrel, or be in anger when praying and praising God.

Lifting up the hands in the case of Moses also meant that he could not use the rod to strike physically as before. It meant total surrender to the will and purpose of God. It meant for Moses, as for us, that he could no longer resort to relying on his rod to hit the rock—it was total surrender.

When we lift up our hands to God, it is in total surrender to the mighty abilities of God, rather than our abilities, which may seem so real to us. God is mighty—*omnipotent, omniscient,* and *omnipresent,* and we should trust Him to help us and to work on our behalf.

TED THEODORE

EXTENDING YOUR GIFTS/POTENTIAL

2 Kings 4, Matthew 14:15, John 2:1-9

G OD'S ORIGINAL INTENT, which has not changed by the way, is to have man live out the image He created him for, i.e. the image of God (Gen. 1:26). To make this possible and a reality for man, God had to bless him. Note that this was the original plan, and you could argue that was the only blessing God gave to us directly.

MANIFESTING THE GIFTS/POTENTIAL IN YOU—I

Blessed be the God and Father of our Lord Jesus Christ, who hath
blessed us with all spiritual blessings in heavenly places in Christ.

(Eph. 1:3)

G OD HAS ALREADY blessed us, that is, He has given us the
empowerment, the ability to prosper—it's already with us. This
is why we say that we are blessed in spiritual places in Christ Jesus.

The ability to get wealth is in you, same as the ability to have children,
to increase in whatever you do. The question is how well are you using it?

Once you stop unleashing you potential, once you stop harvesting, the
harvest stops—it does not mean the field is barren, but your hands and
maybe your faith is lazy or slack.

A slothful man hideth his hand in his bosom, and will not so
much as bring it to his mouth again.

(Prov. 19:24)

Note that the slothful man had his hand in the bosom—a source of
goodness—or had a substance meant for the mouth, but could not bring
it back to his mouth.

So we see the potential and we see the harvest, but nothing happens.

Why is this person described as slothful here? It was possibly because he
could not eat or reap what was set before him, whether it was set before him
or he set it himself. It only proves the point that the slothful man had the
ability to create wealth, i.e. to put food on his table—whether by themselves
or by other people; what he could *not* do was eat to exploit that potential.

It may even be possible that he did not take his hands back to his mouth
because there were people watching, and he did not want people to feel
jealous or envious about the blessings of God. We are called to eat of the
fullness of the land and of the fruit of our labour—nothing shall stop us.

MANIFESTING THE GIFTS/POTENTIAL IN YOU—II

A NOTHER EXAMPLE OF the slothful sowing is given below.

> I went by the field of the slothful, and by the vineyard of the man void of understanding; And, lo, it was all grown over with thorns, and nettles had covered the face thereof, and the stone wall thereof was broken down. Then I saw, and considered it well: I looked upon it, and received instruction. Yet a little sleep, a little slumber, a little folding of the hands to sleep: So shall thy poverty come as one that travelleth; and thy want as an armed man.
>
> (Prov. 24:30-34)

The sluggard had a field, *not a tiny plot*. So probably he had sown in that land. This is because the Bible described it as overgrown with thorns, which meant that there may have been something growing there before. This is atypical of one of the parables of Jesus where he talks about a man who sowed his seeds, and at night as they slept, the enemy came in and sowed in tares (weeds).

The slothful man's challenge was watching over his seed and getting ready for the harvest and actually reaping his crops. The Bible describes thorns in a field as the cares of this world—so the slothful really looks and cares more about the cares of this world than watching and praying over his seed. He is in fact described in Proverbs 24:20 as a '. . . man void of understanding' of the laws of sowing and reaping.'

Actually in Proverbs 26:13, the slothful person gives another excuse for his inability to reap, saying the lion in the street stops them from going to harvest. What stops us from fully exploring our potential and gift is not just slothfulness. It is also courage or a lack of courage or plain old timidity and lack of an understanding of our rights in Christ that stops us from fully partaking of our harvest.

Hosea 4:6 tells us that people (the blessing, the potential) perish for lack of vision and knowledge. No wonder the cemetery is said to be the richest place because people perish with their gifts—for lack of vision/ knowledge.

In Luke 15:31, the elder brother is told that he owns everything that the father owns. The father was just working for him. So, in reality, the gift that the father gave the prodigal son on his return was the eldest son's property. The elder son did *not receive because he did not ask!*

MANIFESTING THE GIFTS/POTENTIAL IN YOU—III

IN 2 KINGS 4, the oil stopped flowing after the last drum was filled. Why did she not bring more jars? Imagine the ridicule of asking for jars in a time when there was no rain, and maybe that is why she did not ask for more.

Yet, even when the oil stopped flowing, I believe that anointing was still upon her, but she did not actualise it any further.

The disciples had the same experience in John 2 (wedding in Cana) and Matthew 14 during the feeding of the 5,000. On both occasions, when they stopped sharing, I believe the anointing was still there, but they stopped.

In 2 Kings 13:18-20, Joash still had the anointing on him when he stopped shooting the arrows, and that is *why* Elisha was angry with him. He failed to use the transferred anointing, which Elisha took with him to the grave (verse 20). No wonder a dead man was raised after falling into Elisha's grave.

Today, Jesus has blessed us with all spiritual blessings. You have the potential—where are you today with your harvest and your victory?

SINNING HABITUALLY?

1 John 2:1

CHRIST OUR INTERCESSOR is also the risen Lamb of God, without sin. He is also the head of the church, which makes us part of His body.

Therefore, if one part of His body (i.e. one of us) keeps on sinning, it means He will have to be presenting that part of Him before God every time because He is the Righteous One—so no unrighteousness can abide in Him.

Thus we need to stop sinning, especially habitually. We cannot claim to be in Christ and be sinning habitually.

> If we claim to be in him, we must walk as Jesus did—for this is
> how we know him.
>
> (1 John 2:5)

INSIDE-OUTSIDE PARADIGM

IN THE NATURAL world, when I wash my car or dishes, especially if they are also dirty on the outside, I usually will start from the inside. This is because I do not want to use the dirt from the outside to stain the inside—especially if I am using the same sponge. If I had to make a choice about where to put my priority, then it would be to focus on the inside only. It is important to have the outside of the car clean, but it is more important to have the inside where all of the actions happen clean. How embarrassing it is for people to really desire to be close to you because of your 'outside'—be that a car, home, clothes, perfume—and when they get close to you . . . and your inside stinks. Jesus was very strong on this in Matthew 23:27-28 when He referred to the Pharisees and all those who share the same traits as whitewashed tombs. In Jeremiah 17:10, the Lord makes it clear that He is interested in the heart, the inside, and not so much the outside. What is in your inside today, and how is that light shining out to others?

HUMILITY IS A CHOICE

Jesus said, 'I tell you the truth, no servant is greater than his master, nor is a messenger greater than the one who sent him.'

(John 13:16)

JESUS MADE THIS statement after telling them that they should be as humble as He had been, by washing their feet. I would imagine that this was a tall order for the disciples—to wash each other's feet. How were they going to do this without people taking them for a ride . . . to upstage them? This same concern goes through a lot of our minds when we think of not serving others.

Jesus had to make this emphatic statement, which is not to say that the servant will not be greater at some point in the future. It is saying that as you do this act of servitude, you do not exchange your positions; rather you reinforce your leadership expression in the eyes of Christ. This is the expression of love: Love does not boast (1 Cor. 13:4). Love is not proud and it is kind. This is leading in love and love never fails (1 Cor. 13:8).

What is most amazing about this act is the timing. On the night that Jesus knew He was going to be crucified with all the sacrifice that was attached to it, He was still focused enough to display this selfless act. For one thing, it shows it was truly in His nature. The reason I say so is that it is at the point of pressure that we usually will be most challenged to show love and other Christian virtues . . . and under pressure (at this time) was love, service, and humility.

EXPLORE . . . PUSH YOUR BOUNDARIES

CALEB WAS EIGHTY-FIVE years old when he asked Joshua to redeem the promise of God to him after forty-five years had passed.

What is peculiar about this story amongst other facts is that Caleb also asked to climb a mountain and to go to war at that age!

Often and again, it is common to see people settle into a routine, after a few years of their lives, and the adventurous ceases to exist. It is, as it were, that learning has stopped, and really there is no point in stretching one's ability any more.

What Caleb was doing in my view was instinctively (and maybe he knew!) responding to the call and purpose of God for all of mankind. God's original intent and commission to man was to be fruitful, replenish the earth, and have dominion over it. Unless we have that spirit and courage to leave our *terra familiaria* and seek opportunity and new experiences, we would never fulfil that purpose of God. To actually dominate the earth, to actually push the frontiers of our experiences, we need to stop being staid and plain, we need to push the boundaries a little bit more.

I believe we would enjoy life more if we explored the unknown a little bit more—the reason I feel so is that we would actually be obeying God's command of dominating the earth. How would we be fruitful if we do not replenish, and how can we replenish if we don't dominate? Dominion is an end point or at least some steps away from being inquisitive, stepping out, and exploring beyond our boundaries.

How can we find out our true potential if we remain staid, doing the same old things the same way all the time? God wants us at the end of our lives to be able to say like Paul (and Caleb), 'I have run the race. I have finished my course . . .'

Step out today and do what you were never able to do
or have simply never tried. Push your boundaries!

THE MANIFEST PRESENCE

Acts 4

PETER AND JOHN had just been arrested for preaching to the people after the healing of the lame man at the Beautiful Gate and were arraigned in court before the high priests and the Sadducees.

In verse 8, the Bible records that the Holy Spirit came upon them, leading and guiding them as they began to respond to the charges before the court. By the time they finished their response in verse 13, the high priest and the Sadducees were convinced that these men had something uncommon about them, that they had been with Jesus: 'When they saw the courage of Peter and John and realised that they were unschooled, ordinary men, they were astonished and they took note that these men had been with Jesus'. This was apparent, given the following:

a) Wisdom with which they spoke, their boldness and unfettered eloquence.
b) Evidence, the miracle (verse 14)—the healed man was standing there.

In the life of a believer, when these conditions are manifest, the following occurs:

a) They yield control to the Holy Spirit—not in part, but in whole.
b) They are not constrained by their education, circumstances (physical or otherwise).
c) They know the move of God and submit themselves to the Holy Spirit.

Then the manifest presence of God becomes obvious to men, and God gets the glory.

In 1 Samuel 10, in the story of Saul, these conditions are present, and the presence of the Lord was made manifest. (a) The spirit came upon him (verse 11), and he prophesied (c) that He was to make (publicly) the king of Israel and God wanted to show him His manifest presence as a sign (verse 9).

God wants to manifest His glory, wisdom, and excellence through us on earth and we need to have these three conditions in our lives. The issue is not per se about the challenges of life and the circumstances we need to deal with. It is more about us acknowledging that God has a move on the earth and committing ourselves to that move. It is yielding to the direction and instruction of the Holy Spirit and in the same vein recognising that in and of ourselves we are inadequately prepared for the task if we had to use our natural abilities.

Let our inadequacies of education, pedigree, etc. not hinder us—rather let our connectedness to God propel and encourage us to be vessels of His Manifest Presence.

BRIGHTER AND BRIGHTER

Enter not into the path of the wicked, and go not in the way of evil men. Avoid it, pass not by it, turn from it, and pass away. For they sleep not, except they have done mischief; and their sleep is taken away, unless they cause some to fall. For they eat the bread of wickedness, and drink the wine of violence. But the path of the just is as the shining light, that shineth more and more unto the perfect day.

(Prov. 4:14-18)

The Bible tells us that God promises us, 'The path of the just is as the shining light, that shineth more and more unto the perfect day'

(Prov. 4:18).

TO UNDERSTAND THIS promise and enter into its reality each day of your life, we need to go into a couple of verses to put it into some context. In verse 14, we are cautioned not to enter into the path of the wicked . . . So there is a path of the wicked, just as there is a path of the just/righteousness, and for both or either paths, there is an entrance and a way to get in. In verses 16 and 17, we see the process or pattern for entering into the path of the wicked—when we eat the bread of wickedness, drink the drink of violence, do mischief . . .

So, just as there is a process for getting into the path of the wicked, there is a way and a process to get your path and your day to be brighter and brighter.

In Psalm 119:105 we are reminded, 'The word of God is a lamp unto our feet and a light into our path'. The Word of God is the means to light up the path of the just. In the same way that we use the torch light to see in the darkness or use the dip and full beams in cars, to regulate the light and brightness around us, so we can use the Word of God.

This promise of our pathway shining brighter into the perfect day does not just happen by itself. It is one of those promises that we can fully tap into when we follow the process. The more the Word we get into our lives, the more our pathway shines. Yes, indeed the Word is a light and a lamp unto our feet, and to get more of that light, to see every corner and dark place, and to get a revelation of everything before us, we need to get in more words into our lives.

To be sure, just by *not* doing the evil acts of the wicked, our paths will shine, but it will not shine as much as it should without a constant infusion of the Word of God: more words, more light, more shine. We can activate that brightness each day as the Holy Spirit illuminates our eyes and our paths by the Word we take in. Amen.

> 'For my thoughts are not your thoughts, neither are your ways my ways,' declares the LORD. As the heavens are higher than the earth, so are my ways higher than your ways and my thoughts than your thoughts.
>
> (Isa. 55:8-9)

In Isaiah 55:8-9, God told the children of Israel that His thoughts were different from their thoughts and their ways were lower than His ways. That was possible or feasible at that time, given their state of relationship with the Lord. Same conditions may apply today if you are not in fellowship with God.

Sometimes we quote this in false humility (*but really in foolishness*) to explain why something happened to us. We imagine we are minions, and this Almighty, Omniscient God is just so far away that it is impossible to know His mind. But Christ came to reveal the will of God, to make plain the Father. 'If you have seen me, you have seen the Father.' Christ came so that we might be one with God—think His thoughts, know His way, and do His will.

That is why in John 15, God says, '. . . if you abide in me and my word abides in you, . . . I and my Father will come and live with you make our home with you'. *So how can God's* thoughts be your thoughts? The real issue is whether His Word is in you, in the inside of you? That is when His ways become your ways and His thoughts your thoughts. The real issue is: Is His Word in you?

In Amos 3:3 we read, 'Can two walk together except they be agreed?' If your walk is different from His walk, it is not because it is hidden; it is because we have been too lazy or not diligent or interested enough to find out. Ask and ye shall receive. Seek and ye shall find. Knock and it shall be opened unto you—all of this is in reference to knowing Him and the power of His Word.

Even in the Old Testament, in Isaiah 30:20-21, God promised to show them the way to walk, the way to prosper.

> Although the Lord gives you the bread of adversity and the water of affliction, your teachers will be hidden no more; with your own eyes you will see them. Whether you turn to the right or to the left, your ears will hear a voice behind you, saying, 'This is the way; walk in it.'

The issue is not with the definition; the issue is with the pathway, the road, and the process of getting there. If you get on the wrong road, you will always arrive at the wrong destination. If you are not getting as blessed, as you would like to be, the issue is not with the blessing; it is with what you are basing your blessings on.

If your thoughts and will are not in line with God's will, then prospering in life would be left to chance. In Joshua 1:6-8, Joshua tells us how to be sure about the road to prosperity. It is true that God's ways and thoughts may be different from ours. However, that line of thinking should rather make us want to join up our thinking with God rather than apologise for it and make excuses for one's inadequacies.

How can we ever hope to enjoy our lives as Christians when we do not talk regularly to God when His presence seems so far away (*indeed His commands are not grievous*). It is like a couple who never really communicate. Indeed a wife who does not talk or spend time regularly with her husband or vice versa finds it is increasingly impossible to enjoy the fullness of that husband, and our husband is Christ.

Abraham had to leave Haran before God could expose the fullness of His plan for him. This is not because God could not bless him there, nor was it because God's blessings (the end/fruit of the journey) was not present when he called Abraham in Haran, but he had to get Abram to a place where he could get his thinking in line with God's thinking—so that he could come into the fullness of God's plans for him. Going to Egypt, lying about Sarah, etc. was because he had not lined up his thinking with God's thinking as yet.

How do we make God's ways our way? It is by doing His Word. James 1:22-24 tells us that if we are only hearers, we deceive ourselves. The way into the fullness of God's blessings is to hear, read, meditate, and *do* the Word. The proof of our belief is in our action.

The Holy Spirit in us is the revealer of the will of God to us. Also, when we pray in tongues, we pray and get into His will. God wants to change our thinking first before He fully manifests Himself—for 'as a man thinketh in his heart, so he is'.

> For with the heart man believeth and with the mouth confession
> is made unto salvation.
>
> (Rom. 10:10)

If your heart cannot believe it, your mouth will not confess, and your eyes will never experience it.

Make God's way your way today.

PREPARING FOR ASSURED SUCCESS

Isaiah 55:10-14

I N ISAIAH 55:8-9, God reminded His people that His thoughts were higher than their thoughts and that they had to line up their thinking with His thinking to be able to benefit from Him and indeed to walk with Him. It is only when we have lined up our thoughts with His Word and ways that we can even began to understand what His thoughts are.

In Genesis 1:26, God signalled His intention to make man after His own image, and that is what He did. This image was to be of the same kind and type as the one from which he was created—the same image of God.

Every time God creates and does this by His Word, we see evidence of this in Genesis 1, Hebrews 11, and John 1. God sends His Word ahead so that the future is prepared for that which the Word is to accomplish.

As things grow in a natural world, there are some conditions to make growth and sustenance possible spiritually. In Genesis 2:5, the Bible tells us that there was no plant/herb growing because there was no rain upon earth. However, there was a mist that went up from the earth, watered the earth causing things to grow (verse 6-8).

In Isaiah 55:1-11, the Lord began to explain this principle in its entirety to us. God likens and typifies the rain, which prepares and sustains the ground, to His Word—that as the rain is, so is the Word going forth and not returning back/void to Him, but ensures that the purpose is established. The seed is sown, grows, and brings a harvest. The main thing that makes that process happen is the rain/water from heaven.

God is therefore saying that before you even sow your seed or know if ever you are going to sow a seed in that area, please water the ground. Use my Word, just as the rain, to know when you can profitably sow and profitably reap!

Germination into the fullness of the manifestation of God's prosperity is through sowing in faith. Without faith, the seed cannot grow in a soil.

So with the early rain, the harvest will not be bountiful without the latter rain.

John 1:1-3 tells us that there is nothing *made* that was *made* without the Word. Note that it says that things will be made, *but how it will be made* depends on whether it is rooted in the Word of God. The fact that you see it being made does not mean it will serve for a long time.

In 1 Kings 18, the Bible tells us that there was no rain and therefore no harvest. It does not mean to say that folks were not sowing . . . but there was no harvest!

It is possible to sow on unfertile ground—a ground that has not been subjected to the Word of God. To override the influence and impact of the unfertile ground, we need the Word of God in that land or aspect of your life before sowing.

In the areas you have sown and not seen results or have not been able to harvest, God is asking you today: 'Which word did you sow alongside?' How did you prepare the ground with the early and latter rain (Jer. 5:24, Joel 2:23)?

In Hebrews 11:3, we understand that 'the world was framed by the word of God'. This means that God determined the extent before He started. It means God declared the end from the beginning. He set the boundaries, He sent in the early rain (*word*) and the latter rain (*word*) to prepare the world for what He was creating, and then He started. Set your frame around your family, your seed/harvest, your housing project, your peace, your health, your job, your children's future.

Death and life are in the power of the tongue. By your words, you are framing your life or your death—the extent of the fullness of your life. Once you have framed your world, God watches over His Word to bring it to pass in your life (Jer. 1:12). God is hastening His Word to bring it to pass in your life.

The problem is not with your seed financially, your labour (of love), your generosity, and your faith (even) . . . It may be with your rain of *words*, your framing, and the consistency thereof.

WHAT ARE YOU DOING?

What do you think? There was a man who had two sons. He went to the first and said, 'Son, go and work today in the vineyard.' 'I will not,' he answered, but later he changed his mind and went. Then the father went to the other son and said the same thing. He answered, 'I will, sir,' but he did not go. 'Which of the two did what his father wanted?' 'The first,' they answered.

(Matt. 21:28-31)

IN JAMES 1:22-23 and Luke 6:47, the Lord emphasises the primacy of doing and of taking action over merely listening to the Word of God. God is more interested in what we do than in what we hear because what we do is the proof that we actually heard or actually believed what we heard. Recall that Jesus told the story of two children who were asked to do something. The one He commended was the one who said 'no' but did 'yes' (i.e. did what the father requested).

In fact, James says when we hear only, we deceive ourselves. In the world of (organisational) learning, we would say (true) that learning only occurs after the action is taken.

What we do is so important because they can negate or propel our harvest. You can frame the world all you want with your Word, but if you do not step out in faith, you will be like the sluggard, who cannot put the food in their mouth. It's like saying *put your money where your mouth is*. In fact both should be in the same place—rowing in the same direction.

In Matthew 5:23-24, Jesus deepens this principle by saying that giving (sowing) whilst you are in strife does not please God. Yes, you know the Word; yes, you have even confessed it, but are you living the Word, preparing the grounds, by not living in strife?

But let's step back a bit to understand more the importance of what we hear and who we hear from especially as that often informs our actions.

Psalm 1:1 talks about not *walking*, not taking action, *not* doing things after the counsel of the ungodly. Now what is ungodly counsel? Ungodly means 'unlike God', not like God, not in the character of God, not in the image of God. It does not matter who is saying it; the test is . . . does it line up with the Word of God (Luke 6:45-46). After all, Jesus rebuked the devil when Simeon was the actual speaker; the old prophet gave counsel to the young prophet, contrary to the Word of God.

Test every spirit and see if they are of God. By their fruit you shall know them. What bears fruit in you is not per se what you hear, it is what you believe; it is what you meditate on day and night. It is not what comes out from others that counts; it is what goes into you—what you allow to come out of you.

The reason the ungodly are blown away like chaff by the Word is that they are walking outside God's counsel. Their lives have not been stabilised by the Word of God. The wind described or referred to in Psalm 1:4 is akin to the storm and wind in Luke 6:47-49. Same rain, same storm came upon both houses, but only one house survived.

Chaff (doctrine, philosophy, and way of life) is blown because it is not rooted in God's ways. Where you stand, or whether you are standing after a (challenging) event, is the proof of whether you are grounded or not.

In Psalm 1:6, God says that He knows the way of the righteous because He orders the footsteps of the righteous. In Psalm 119:9, 105, we know that when we obey God's Word, we walk in His way; therefore, when the wind blows we know we shall not be blown away, when the waters come we shall not be overwhelmed, and when the fire passes through we shall not be burnt or singed . . . because we walk in God's ways, because we obey and do His will.

It is when your body cells are weak or inadequate that you notice (more than other folks) that the weather is colder and the air is not pure enough. It is not the wind that is strong . . . . It is your body that is weak. Proverbs 24:10 says, 'If you faint in the day of adversity, then your strength is small'.

So take comfort in the fact that no matter what happens, God says He will never leave you, not forsake you, as long as you are walking in His will, doing His Word, obeying His command. He will be the fourth man in the fire for/with you.

Obedience is better than sacrifice and to hearken (listen) than the fat of rams. Obey whether it makes sense to you or not. Obey because it is God's Word, not based on who said it or on your judgement of what it says. Be like the Berean Christian who searched out the Word of God.

When you hear counsel or people tell you things contrary to God's Word, speak back God's Word to the situation, just as Jesus declared God's Word to the devil.

Stand (on God's Word) and see the salvation of God manifest in every area of your life.

YOUR EYES SET THE LIMIT

S AMUEL HAD A message from God for Saul.

> Samuel said, 'Although you were once small in your own eyes, did you not become the head of the tribes of Israel? The LORD anointed you king over Israel.'
>
> (1 Sam. 15:17)

Saul could never have been king if he was left to his own devices. He could not see himself as king, even if the opportunity was presented to him without the Word and the man of God present.

If you were to decide your destiny, you may become either an Absalom or a Saul. Absalom tried to be king because people told him he looked like one, talked like one, acted more like a king than his father and he believed them! Saul, on the other hand, became a king but truly did not know what was inside him; he did not upgrade his thinking. There are lizards in king's palaces.

There are two phases in the creation of a thing—there is the conceptual (spiritual) and there is the manifestation (physical). The former determines the latter. There is no way you will go beyond your dreams, your vision of yourself, where you came from, what people say about you until you key into what God says about you.

David responded to a situation in his life, saying, 'I have been young and now an old. I have never seen the righteous forsaken, nor his seed begging bread.' (*Mephiboseth, Jonathan's son, did beg, but not for long because he was in covenant with the righteous.*)

Greater is He that is in you than He that is in the world. What does 'greater' mean to you?

Whatsoever is born of God overcomes the world, even our faith. If the first creation is not born of God, it can never overcome obstacles of the second creation. The force of manifestation is in the creative source.

How do you see?

- By what you read, what you hear, what you have seen before, what people have said about you, etc.
- Until you know what is yours, you cannot claim it. You may be passing and overlooking your own property because you cannot see it.
- Your peace, your wealth may be eluding you because you cannot see that it is yours. Just like the presents under the Christmas tree, you cannot tell which is yours and what is inside unless you are extremely sure about your parents' love for you.

We have been given a *name* above every other name (Jesus); at the name of Jesus, every knee should bow and every tongue confess that Jesus is Lord. But what really is in that name that should make every knee bow and every tongue confess?

How well do you know that name?

DESIRE THE PURGING OF GOD

John 15:2-3

WE ARE IN the vine. Jesus is the vine. God is the husbandman, the vine dresser. When it is time for more fruits, the vine dresser purges us. When I think about the action of purging, I think about a pipe that is partially clogged. Until it is fully de-clogged or purged, it can only produce a limited amount of fruit and glory.

In verse 3, God, the vine dresser, tells us that the way to de-clog and purge is through applying the Word to our lives. So what that means is that there are times when God will be purging us so that we could produce more fruit. At times like that, we do not necessarily produce fruit. Rather, those are the times that we get ready for the next big release of God's glory in our lives. Ecclesiastes says that there is a time for sowing and a time for reaping. We must be willing to go through the 'purging'.

Purging is not necessarily a bad or painful thing, at least not the way it sounds. It really is getting God's Word into your life to cleanse out all the unbelief, doubt, fear-based thoughts that the devil would have sown in our lives through the media, colleagues, etc. If you recall the parable of the sower, the devil is always trying to pollute our fruit-bearing abilities. There we should consciously seek out God's Word every now and then so that our pipes are cleansed out and ready to bear great fruit to God's glory. Verse 8 tells us that God is glorified when we bear much fruit. So it is only when we have our vessels full and free that we can bear much fruit to God's glory.

Would you take time out to purge yourself today and this week?

Lightning Source UK Ltd.
Milton Keynes UK
UKOW050028100112

185054UK00001B/77/P